Tales from the Saints Sideline

Jeff Duncan

SP
SPORTS
PUBLISHING
L.L.C.

www.SportsPublishingLLC.com

Director of production: Susan M. Moyer
Acquisitions editor: Scott Musgrave
Project manager: Jim Henehan
Dust jacket design: Dustin Hubbart
Developmental editor: Doug Hoepker
Copy editor: Cynthia L. McNew
Photo editor: Erin Linden-Levy
Marketing manager: Mike Hagan

ISBN: 1-58261-770-8

Printed in the United States of America

Sports Publishing L.L.C.
www.sportspublishingllc.com

This book is dedicated to my wonderful parents:
my mother, who taught me a love of words;
and my father, who taught me a love of sports.

CONTENTS

FOREWORD

I have seen it all.

In 37 years of chronicling Saints football, there's not much left to experience.

Name it in Saints football, and I was there. Ernie Pyle and Bob Woodward have nothing on me.

I was there for John Gilliam's return and Randy Mueller's exit.

I covered Tom Dempsey's kick and John Carney's miss.

I witnessed the Bag Heads and the Benson Boogie.

In almost four decades of chronicling the lovable Fleur de Lis, I've traversed the country to training camps in Point Loma, California, Vero Beach, Florida, Hammond, Louisiana, Thibodaux, Louisiana, Ruston, Louisiana, and LaCrosse, Wisconsin, endured horrible songs like "Big Bad Bum" and "Take It to the Top" and survived the world premiere of "Number One."

I've raced an ostrich at halftime and watched Fetch Monster work on kickoffs.

I have seen greats like Archie Manning, Tommy Myers, Rickey Jackson, Sam Mills, Willie Roaf and Deuce McAllister.

I have typed the names Jubilee Dunbar, D'Artagnan Martin, Cephus Weatherspoon, Bivian Lee, Happy Feller, Guido Merkens, and Ink Aleaga into my typewriter and laptop.

I buckled at Big Ben, revered at The River City Relay and called 9-1-1 on Joe Horn's "Cell-ebration."

I've hummed to "Who Dat?" and chuckled at "Cha-ching."

And throughout it all, I've marveled at every madcap minute of it.

Tales from the Saints Sideline relives the greatest stories in franchise history—and reveals dozens of never before heard ones. It's a comprehensive compilation of one of the most colorful and compelling franchises in sports.

Sure, the 49ers and Cowboys have the championships. The Packers and the Bears have the tradition. But has Ben Hur ever portrayed one of their quarterbacks in a movie? The Saints have the stories. Read on and see what I mean.

Enjoy.

Peter Finney
The Times-Picayune

ACKNOWLEDGMENTS

This project would not have been possible without the assistance of dozens of friends, colleagues and associates. Without their efforts, I would have failed worse than the 1980 Saints.

I'd like to recognize some key contributors:

My supervisors at *The Times-Picayune*—including sports editor David Meeks, assistant sports editor Doug Tatum, executive editor Jim Amoss and publisher Ashton Phelps—must be thanked for allowing me the time and opportunity to pursue this project and for patiently listening to my endless harping about it.

Saints media relations director Greg Bensel and tireless assistants Justin Macione, Ricky Zeller and Nick Karl deserve recognition for their help with records, research and contacts.

Times-Picayune mentors Peter Finney and Bob Roesler advised me on the joys and evils of being a first-time author.

Colleagues Brian Allee-Walsh, Jim Rapier and Bob Warren of *The Times-Picayune,* Sheldon Mickles of *The (Baton Rouge) Advocate* and Scott Beder of *The (Monroe) News-Star* are thanked for their valued input.

New Orleans sports historian Bob Remy's knowledge, interest and contributions to this project are also appreciated.

I am indebted to *Times-Picayune* photo editor Doug Parker, *Times-Picayune* ace photographer Alex Brandon and the incredibly talented photo staff at *The Times-Picayune* for their contributions.

Saints Hall of Fame director Ken Trahan and WWL radio show host Kaare Johnson provided assistance with contact information.

And last but certainly not least, the countless players, coaches and front office executives who contributed their time and efforts in making this book a reality cannot be overlooked. I hope this book is a fond and accurate reflection of your memories.

CHAPTER 1

The Inaugural Season

Dave Dixon

There wouldn't be a New Orleans Saints if it weren't for Dave Dixon.

It was Dixon who came up with the nickname "Saints."

It was Dixon who organized the preseason and all-star games that allowed New Orleans to showcase its fanatical following of professional football.

It was Dixon who campaigned around the state for the construction of a new stadium to help lure the team.

It was Dixon who later named that building The Superdome.

Dixon's dreams, and those of New Orleans sports fans far and wide, were realized on All Saints Day, November 1, 1966.

Before an overflow crowd at the Pontchartrain Hotel, NFL commissioner Pete Rozelle officially announced the decision to award the city of New Orleans the league's 16th franchise.

The New Orleans team would be an expansion club, following the path of recent additions in Atlanta (1966), Minnesota (1961) and Dallas (1960).

"It all started some five years ago when David Dixon started hounding our league meetings," Rozelle said of the man known as "The father of New Orleans' professional football dream."

Dinner at Antoine's

In 1965, New Orleans was a very different place. Especially for a black man. The passage of the Civil Rights Act had occurred only a few months earlier. Before that, 21 black players boycotted an AFL All-Star game in New Orleans because of the way they were treated in the city before the game.

The boycott concerned Pete Rozelle. The NFL commissioner was intent on expanding into the deep South. He had awarded the league's 15th franchise to Atlanta and was considering locating a franchise in New Orleans.

"It was just unfortunate to have occurred in New Orleans," Dixon said. "New Orleans is a melting pot of ethnic cultures, a city renowned for its predominantly live-and-let-live attitudes."

Rozelle sent Buddy Young, a former running back at Illinois and the Baltimore Colts, to visit the city as a representative. Rozelle asked Dixon to take Young to one of the city's finest restaurants. Dixon called Antoine's, one of the most famous and historic restaurants in the French Quarter.

"I called the proprietor at Antoine's and told him what I wanted to do," Dixon said. "He said, 'It's time. Let's get it done.'"

Dixon and Young sat at a table in the main dining room, where Young was the only ethnic face in the crowd.

Dixon could feel the steely stares of his fellow diners. Across the way, he spied an acquaintance he knew privately harbored racist views. The man was staring at their table. Dixon could sense an impending altercation.

"The man finally got up, walked over to our table and went straight to Buddy," Dixon said. "My heart was pounding. I was sure he was going to make a scene that would cost us any chance of getting an NFL team."

Instead of an insult, the interloper offered a question.

"He said, 'Aren't you Buddy Young?'" Dixon said.

Young said he was.

"I'm an Illini man," the man said. "I watched you all the time when you played for us. You're the greatest running back I have ever seen. I'm a big fan."

The man and Young enjoyed each other's company as if they were long, lost pals.

"I could have half-died right there," Dixon said.

Young returned to New York and gave Rozelle a glowing report on the city.

Twenty-two months later, New Orleans was awarded the NFL's 16th franchise.

Name Game

Dave Dixon never had a doubt as to what New Orleans' new professional football team should be named.

"It was Saints all the way," Dixon said.

Indeed, Dixon had championed the name since he began his campaign for a pro team in 1963. He even ordered boxes of "New Orleans Saints" pencils and handed them out to anyone who'd take them.

Despite Dixon's efforts, The *States-Item* started a "name the team" contest shortly after Pete Rozelle officially awarded a team to the city in 1966. The paper was swamped with dozens of entries. Deltas. Jazz Kings. Tarpons. Jazzers. Tigers. Nolas. Blues. Domes. Crescents. Ramparts. Crawfish. Skippers. Stevedores. Mudbugs.

Each had earned mention in the *States-Item*'s "name the team" contest. But Dixon said the contract was strictly window dressing.

"It was a boat race all along," Dixon said.

Dixon came up with the name after the song "When the Saints Go Marchin' In," made famous by jazz great Louis Armstrong.

"How can you pass up the opportunity to have free advertising 365 days a year?" Dixon said. "It's as simple as that. Once I zeroed in on that, I said there can't be any other name."

Still, new owner John Mecom was leery. He was concerned that some fans would take offense to the religious reference. He sent one of his public relations executives to New Orleans to try to talk Dixon out of the name. Dixon refused to budge.

His fears were quelled a short time later during a chance meeting at a local restaurant with Archbishop Philip M. Hannan.

"I was horrified for what I'd done, so I stopped him and got up and apologized," Dixon said. "I told him some gentlemen think somehow or another the name 'Saints' for our football team might be a little sacrilegious. The archbishop replied, 'Oh, my God, no! It's certainly not sacrilegious. Besides, I have a terrible instinct that we're going to need all the help we can get.' That sealed the name Saints forever. Little did he know how right he was!"

John Mecom

John Mecom Jr. was the Mark Cuban of his day, a dashing 27-year-old Texan who inherited millions from his father's oil empire.

On December 15, 1966, NFL commissioner Pete Rozelle awarded ownership of the Saints to Mecom and his 18-man investment group in a bidding war that involved four other groups. Mecom paid $8.5 million for the club.

One of Mecom's first orders of business was to select the team colors. He favored blue and yellow, while local newspaper columnists tried to sway him toward red, white and blue. He eventually settled on black and gold, appropriately, considering the fortune his family made in the "black gold" business.

Mecom came to the Saints with a reputation as a deep-pocketed playboy. He was accustomed to luxury and its accoutrements. Among his largesse were 12 airplanes, two helicopters, three ocean-going vessels, two Colorado ranches, another spread in Laredo, Texas, with its own landing strip, several mansions in Houston and a personal suite in the Waldorf-Astoria Hotel in New York City.

John's Island

At 27, John Mecom Jr. was the youngest owner in the league, younger than many of his players. The husky 6-4, 200-pounder played middle guard as a freshman at the University of Oklahoma and was often mistaken for a player by fans at early Saints practices. Off the field, Mecom mixed in just as smoothly.

Stars Paul Hornung and Jim Taylor were counted among his running mates who regularly attended parties on Mecom's luxurious yacht or at his posh condo.

"There was a man named Bill Smyth who had been involved with the Mecoms," former public relations director Don Smith said. "He was on the Saints executive committee, but his real job was to be a watchdog for John Jr. He was always around.

"If he oversaw everything John did," Smith added, "he was a busy man."

Saints running back Chuck Muncie recalls attending parties on Mecom's yacht, endearingly referred to as "John's Island" by players and coaches.

"He would have movie stars and actresses and players and coaches on that boat," Muncie said. "He knew how to have a good time."

Mecom was not afraid to mix it up, either. His competitive streak reared its head in the fourth game of the inaugural season.

Saints linebacker Steve Stonebreaker instigated a now-famous bench-clearing brawl at the end of an emotional 27-21 loss to the Giants at Yankee Stadium.

Mecom threw a couple of haymakers in the direction of a pair of Giants players. His arm was thrown out of place during the scuffle.

"I know I shouldn't have been there," Mecom told *The New York Times* afterward. "Somebody took a punch at me. I think it was No. 81 (Freeman White). I got emotional and lost my cool. I threw a punch at No. 81. I missed and hurt my arm."

Front Office Shuffle

Mecom was equally freewheeling with his checkbook. He made a quick splash by signing Jim Taylor away from Green Bay. Taylor was the biggest star in football at the time, and Mecom lured him with a four-year, $400,000 contract to be paid over 20 years. The deal was one of the largest in pro football. Mecom also unloaded a wad of cash to take the team to San Diego for training camp at Cal Western University.

"He could spend some money," said then-Saints quarterback Billy Kilmer. "He had a suite down in San Diego at the Yacht Harbor and they would have some big parties down there. He always had something going on."

Unfortunately, Mecom wasn't as proficient at running a football team. The Saints went though two general managers and three business managers before their first season began. He later hired Richard F. Gordon Jr., a former astronaut with no football experience, as general manager.

Is it any wonder the Saints never had a winning season in Mecom's 19-year tenure?

"Ownership didn't know what they were doing," Kilmer said. "John was a nice guy, but he was just inexperienced, and he didn't hire good people. He kept going through general managers and he never could settle on anyone that was a football man."

"I never had any problem with John Jr., but (director of player personnel) Vic Schwenk, he was out of his mind," Saints defensive end Doug Atkins said. "Vic Schwenk didn't know anything about football. John Jr. hired friends. He got a good one in Coach (Tom) Fears, but a lot of those other people didn't know anything about football or how to run a front office."

Under Mecom, the Saints would go 83-187-3 in 19 seasons before he finally sold the team to Tom Benson on May 31, 1986.

Tom Fears

Shortly after being named owner, John Mecom narrowed his list of head coaching candidates to three men: Tom Fears, Dallas Cowboys defensive coordinator Dick Nolan and UCLA head coach Tommy Prothro. Nolan was considered the favorite because Mecom had already hired former Cowboys secretary-treasurer Bedford Wynn as a vice president.

But Fears won out in part because he wanted the job more than anyone else and also because of his association with legendary Green Bay Packers coach Vince Lombardi. Fears coached on Lombardi's first Packers staff and was credited with implementing the short passing attack that made Bart Starr a star.

Fears was hired on December 27, 1966 and signed a five-year contract that paid him $35,000 a season.

"Fears was a disciple of Lombardi's but he wasn't as gifted as Lombardi," former *Times-Picayune* sports editor Bob Roesler said. "And everyone figured he must be smart if he worked under Lombardi. And that hurt. He was on a pedestal."

Thomas Jesse Fears was the son of a mining engineer father and a Mexican mother. In 1951, he married Luella Wintheiser, a pretty woman of German decent who hailed from Minneapolis. They raised six children, three boys and three girls, who in turn bore six grandchildren.

Fears was a fit and handsome man. During his playing days at UCLA, he worked as a stand-in for Clark Gable in the 1951 western *Across the Wide Missouri*.

On the sideline, Fears was intense and demanding. Ed Staton of *The Times-Picayune* once wrote that Fears was "a guy who could sell elevator shoes to Doug Atkins."

Rebuilding Plan Goes Awry

Having spent the 1966 season on the staff of the expansion Atlanta Falcons, Fears knew the challenge that awaited the Saints.

At his introductory press conference, Fears told reporters he hoped to construct his expansion team the same way the Cowboys and Falcons were molded—by building for the future and not squandering future draft choices for marginal players in the autumn of their careers.

"Although many feel the common draft now makes trading more important, I still maintain you have to build your club by developing your draft choices," Fears said.

The statement proved ominous.

The Saints frivolously traded away three of their four first-round draft picks during his first three seasons. They also dealt away two second-round picks, including one to Los Angeles for draft information.

The first-round picks the Saints dealt in 1967, 1968 and 1969 were used to draft defensive tackle Bubba Smith (Colts), linebacker Fred Carr (Packers) and tight end Ted Kwalick (49ers). Those players combined to earn eight Pro Bowl selections.

And what largesse did Fears reap? An unproven back-up quarterback named Gary Cuozzo, an aging Packers full-back in Jim Taylor and 49ers receiver Dave Parks.

"It was a joke," said Jack Faulkner, Fears' top defensive assistant. "Everybody was involved, from ownership on down. Too many people put their nose in there. You hire a guy, you let him do the job. We had too many advisors."

No Regrets

They say bad things come in threes. Tom Fears would agree.

On the Saints' fourth birthday, All Saints Day, November 1, 1970, they lost to the Rams, 30-17, to fall to 1-5-1. During the halftime show, a re-enactment of the Battle of New Orleans, a cannon misfired, costing one of the participants three fingers. A day later Fears was fired. His final record was 14-34-2.

Trainer Warren Ariail called the dismissal "the greatest injustice since the rape of Nanking."

"I liked Fears and thought he was a good coach," said defensive end Doug Atkins, who played previously in his career for Cleveland's Paul Brown and Chicago's George Halas. "They had a lot of people who thought they were coaches. He had a lot of people cutting his throat."

Fears was diagnosed with Alzheimer's Disease in 1994 and died January 4, 2000. He went to his grave as the only

Saints head coach who improved his win total in each of his first three seasons.

"I used to try to figure out what I could have changed in those early days to have made things better," Fears told *The Times-Picayune* in 1997. "But I've never had any luck."

Mecom's Misfits

They might have been the most loved three-win team in NFL history.

The first Saints team went just 3-11, but it will go down in club history as one of the most memorable seasons.

The roster was stocked through an expansion draft in January.

In the expansion draft, the Saints selected one player from each of the 11-man lists submitted by 14 teams (Atlanta was exempt because it had just joined the league a year earlier). Each team was allowed to pull two players back before the Saints made their remaining two picks. They were not allowed to select more than three players from any team.

The players available to the Saints were a collection of aging veterans, injury suspects and questionable characters. Each prospect came with a scarlet letter.

The cast of characters included Mike "Tilly" Tilleman, Steve "Stoney" Stonebreaker, Roy "Captain Weirdo" Schmidt, Monty "Doctor Strangebrain" Stickles, Billy "Furnace Face" Kilmer and Louie "The Lip" Cordileone.

The 1967 Saints, also known as "Mecom's Misfits." *Photo courtesy of Bob Remy*

Stickles, a tight end from Notre Dame, once was banned for life from the South Bend campus because of improper conduct.

Kilmer earned his nickname because of his ruddy complexion, which many say was due to his fondness for a postgame beer or three.

Doug Atkins was a towering 6-8, 270-pound giant who liked to shoot guns and martinis from a Hurricane glass.

"We were often referred to as 'Boystown on Cleats,'" Stonebreaker once said.

Athletic trainer Warren Ariail had a better moniker: "Mecom's Misfits."

"That team was a bunch of tough guys," Ariail said. "They didn't win a lot of games, but the Saints never lost a fight."

French Quarter Regulars

Director of player personnel Vic Schwenk oversaw the draft. It was a chaotic time for the organization. The front office had three general managers in the 11-month span between the franchise's inauguration in November 1966 and its opening game in September, 1967. Schwenk selected 42 veterans in the expansion draft and added 36 rookies from the common college draft.

"In the 1967 expansion draft, the other teams put every 'dog' that they could on that list," said Jack Faulkner, the defensive coordinator on the first Saints coaching staff. "A lot of those guys didn't stay around very long, and most of them didn't contribute anything. That's the reason all those old guys were out there."

The group was more famous for its work off the field than on it. Many of the players, led by the free-spirited Atkins, Kilmer, Cordileone and Danny Abramowicz, spent their nights and early mornings in French Quarter bars run by Al Hirt and Pete Fountain.

"New Orleans was known as a swinging city in those days, even more than it is now." Former *Times-Picayune* sports editor Bob Roesler said. "The guys liked going down to Bourbon Street and other places. Some of it rubbed off on the players and perhaps on some of the coaches, and winning didn't seem to matter as much as having fun."

False Hope

Surprisingly, the Saints managed to enjoy early success. After dropping their exhibition opener to the Los Angeles Rams, the Saints reeled off five consecutive preseason victories. The success stirred the expectations and passion of New Orleans' football-starved fans.

The preseason win total was the most ever by an expansion team and caused respected Rams coach George Allen to remark, "The Saints are the best expansion I've ever seen at this stage."

Then reality hit. The Saints lost their first seven games and finished at 3-11. But over the course of the season, they fought and scrapped their way into the hearts of Saints fans everywhere and managed to provide some of the most unforgettable memories in club history.

"We had a cast of characters on that team," said Ray Rissmiller, the starting left tackle. "We all were sort of cast off, hurt or injured and needed a new chance. We were all fighting like heck to make it, and we all hung pretty close to each other."

"We had some pretty good players," Atkins said. "We just didn't have enough of 'em."

The First Showtime

Off the field, Mecom's Misfits were a huge hit. The club finished second in the league in attendance with an average of 75,463 for seven dates. The figure was the sixth highest in the history of the NFL. The Saints led the NFL in the sale of pennants, souvenir radios, T-shirts, jewelry, sweaters, plaques and watches.

Thanks to the creative mind of entertainment director Tommy Walker, Saints games were events more than athletic contests.

Legendary trumpeter Al Hirt, who also was a part owner of the team, blared hot jazz from a special stand behind the Saints bench. He would lead cheers with a microphone, barking "Go, Saints, Go" or "Hold That Line," depending who had the ball.

"Gumbo," the team's 200-pound Saint Bernard mascot worked the sidelines bearing a blanket with a huge fleur de lis logo. Traditional New Orleans marching bands —the Olympia, Eureka and Excelsior—accompanied by a second line of costumed merry-goers played during the pregame shows.

Halftime shows featured hot-air balloons, ostrich chariot races and pigeon releases. The elaborate shows ended when a re-enactment of the Battle of New Orleans resulted in a cannon blast that blew off a participant's hand. At one halftime show, a specialist zipped across the stadium wearing a jetpack on his back like Buck Rogers.

Before the first ever game against the Rams, Walker scheduled a balloon take-off to launch the festivities. Hirt accompanied the show by playing "Up, Up and Away" on his trusty trumpet.

Unfortunately, the balloon never took flight. "I went through 10 choruses and that son of a gun still hadn't been pumped up," Hirt later told *The Times-Picayune*. "I almost got a hernia."

An attendant had mistakenly pulled the wrong cord causing a tear to the balloon's red-and-white canopy. The show was quickly aborted.

The comment from the press box: "I hope that's not an omen."

Unfortunately, it was.

Jazz great Al Hirt, right, was one of the 1967 expansion team's top cheerleaders. *Photo courtesy of Bob Remy*

Danny Abramowicz

It was the third week of training camp in 1967, when a brash rookie out of Xavier (Ohio) University was told to turn in his playbook.

Seventh-round draft picks are lucky to make it past the first week of training camp, so coach Tom Fears wasn't concerned about cutting Abramowicz.

The headstrong Abramowicz had other plans.

"I hurried downstairs and walked into Coach Fears's office," Abramowicz said. "Before he could say anything, I said, 'Coach, you're not cutting me. I didn't get a fair chance and I'm not leaving.'"

Stunned by Abramowicz's courage and brashness, Fears relented and gave him another week to make something happen.

The next week, the Saints played a preseason game at Portland, Oregon, against San Francisco. Word of Abramowicz's status had leaked to the team.

"I was starting because it was against my ex-team," quarterback Billy Kilmer said. "I told Danny, 'I'm going to throw you the ball. You better catch it, and you better play your heart out.' He caught all five balls I threw to him and made some big plays on special teams. And that's how he made the team."

Abramowicz eventually won a permanent spot in the starting lineup by catching 12 passes for 156 yards in his first start. He went on to lead the NFL in receiving in 1969 with 73 catches.

Abramowicz was a classic overachiever story. The frail 6-1, 197-pounder was considered too small and too slow by NFL standards.

But Abramowicz quickly won over his teammates with his heart and grit. During an early training camp scrimmage, Abramowicz caught an elbow from Obert Logan. The force of the blow knocked four of Abramowcz's bottom teeth at right angles to his throat. He played most of the rest of the season with his teeth wired in place.

"Danny was a competitor," Kilmer said. "He wasn't the fastest guy in the world and not the biggest guy in the world. But boy, he had a lot of heart and he had great hands."

Those hands helped Abramowicz become the second player in pro football history to catch at least 50 balls a season for each of the first four years of his career. Mike Ditka was the first.

Coach Tom Fears compared Abramowicz to Colts Pro Bowler Ray Berry.

Of Abramowicz, Ed Staton of *The Times-Picayune* once wrote: "You could drop a football full of money down from an airplane into a Canal St. crowd on Mardi Gras and Abramowicz would be the one to catch it."

Abramowicz made 309 catches in five seasons before being traded to San Francisco after a falling out with owner John Mecom Jr. His receiving total still ranks third behind Eric Martin and Joe Horn in club history.

"You don't see receivers like Danny any more," Kilmer said. "He was tough, he ran great patterns and he had a great enthusiasm for the game. You couldn't lose a guy like that. They made the right choice. It was one of the few right choices they made."

Doug Atkins

It's safe to say no one had ever seen anything quite like Doug Atkins when he arrived at Saints camp in the summer of 1967. A mountain of a man, he towered over his teammates and intimidated everyone who crossed his path.

The Saints acquired the 37-year-old Atkins in a trade with Chicago. He had starred the previous 14 seasons in Cleveland and Chicago, earning eight Pro Bowl trips in 12 seasons with the Bears. But in 1967 he was on the downside of his career and had worn out his welcome with "Papa Bear" George Halas, who dealt the disgruntled giant to New Orleans in mid-July.

Ed Staton, who covered the first Saints team for *The Times-Picayune*, wrote after seeing Atkins for the first time, "You said to yourself, this man wasn't born. The Arctic ice cracked, an explosion following, and this awesome 6-8, 270-pounder came out."

Colleague Will Peneguy concurred: "If ever a man was typecast to walk around the beach kicking sand at everyone, Atkins is that man. From his viewpoint the world has been inflicted with an epidemic of anemia."

Atkins was a great player in his heyday, and unlike many of his cast-off teammates, he still had some gas left in the tank when he came to New Orleans. He developed a strong following amongst fans, who called themselves "Atkins' Army."

"When Doug wanted to play, you couldn't block him," Rissmiller said. "He had these huge forearms and he'd pop you with them and just really knock you around. I've seen him jump over tackles and I've seen him go right through them."

Defensive end Doug Atkins was a larger-than-life character on the Saints' first team. *The Times-Picayune*

The Day the Music Died

It was 11 p.m. on a warm August night in San Diego, California. The first-year New Orleans Saints were a couple of weeks into their first training camp at California-Western University.

The coaches had just finished bed check a few minutes earlier when Billy Kilmer settled down for a much-needed rest.

The rookies on the upper floor of the two-story dormitory had other ideas. Their stereo blasted late-night tunes into the sweet California night.

After about 10 minutes of ruckus, Kilmer heard a booming voice roar from one of the first floor windows.

"It was Atkins," Kilmer said. "He said, 'Shut that music off!'"

Nothing happened.

Another protest. It, too, fell on deaf ears.

"I'm almost falling asleep," Kilmer said, "And I hear, 'Pow! Pow! Pow!'"

Kilmer bolted out of bed and raced into the room next door, where Atkins had a shotgun aimed skyward out the window.

"They were up there raising cain, and Coach Fears was pretty good to us, so I just decided it was a little too late for all that noise," Atkins said. "I hollered up there and didn't get a response. I had a screen on the window and couldn't get it off, so I just angled an old .38 (shotgun) out there. We were on that water so those shots echoed like a cannon."

Thankfully no one died. But the music did.

"You could have heard a pin drop," Kilmer said.

Atkins added: "It got just quiet as a mouse. I don't know who was up there, but they shouldn't have been doing all that stuff. It was after curfew."

The next day all the rookies moved down the hall. No one roomed above Atkins for the rest of training camp.

Not-So-Gentle Giant

Before facing Atkins as a member of the 1966 Philadelphia Eagles, Ray Rissmiller remembers the advice center Jim Ringo offered him.

"Ray, when you go against Atkins, whatever you do, don't hold him," Ringo said. "Because if you hold him he's going to hurt me."

A confused Rissmiller asked Ringo why Atkins would hurt him if Rissmiller was the culprit?

"Because," Ringo said, "he's going to pick you up and throw you on me."

Fears wanted to conserve Atkins's energy for game days, so he limited his participation in practices and exhibition games.

When Atkins did practice he usually made an impact.

Tackle Ray Rissmiller was the unlucky soul who had to battle Atkins during drills. He remembers one practice in particular during the Saints' first training camp in San Diego.

"I was blocking Doug in a one-on-one drill, and he caught me good," said Rissmiller, a 6-5, 258-pound tackle. "He squeezed me at the elbows, picked me off the ground, then caught me again. I saw stars. Later that day, Doug told me, 'I'm sorry Ray, but I came out today to throw two licks. You just happened to catch both of 'em.'"

Billy Kilmer

William Orland Kilmer reported to his first mini-camp with the New Orleans Saints in June of 1967. Months earlier, the Saints had rescued him from purgatory as a back-up running back in San Francisco by selecting him in the expansion draft.

Where some saw a dead end, Kilmer saw opportunity.

His career was going nowhere in San Francisco. Of course, he was lucky to be playing football at all. In December of 1962, Kilmer lost control of his car on an off-ramp of a California highway and crashed into a drainage ditch. He sustained a compound fracture in his ankle and developed an infection in the joint after lying unconscious in the stagnant water. Doctors told him he would probably lose his lower left leg.

But Kilmer—and his leg—survived. He missed all of the 1963 season and played only sparingly in the next three seasons.

"I wanted to play quarterback but they needed running backs in San Francisco," Kilmer said. "When I went to New Orleans, I said I'm going to make the most of it. I didn't care who they got as quarterback."

So there was Kilmer on that sweltering June day, reporting to player personnel director George Owen's office.

"I said, 'Here, just give me the contract,'" Kilmer said. "I signed it and threw it back to him. Honest to God I didn't know what I made. All I want is just give me a chance to play. If I can't play, this doesn't mean anything. Money will come later if I can play."

Gary Cuozzo was the anti-Kilmer. A prototype drop-back passer, he was tall, handsome and blessed with picture-perfect form. He also was a bit of a prima donna. With Mecom's Misfits, he might as well have been a leper.

Cuozzo came to the Saints in a March 6 trade with Baltimore. The Saints traded the No. 1 overall pick in the 1967 draft and two players for the former University of Virginia signal caller who rarely played as Johnny Unitas's back-up.

Fears gave Cuozzo every chance to win the job, but he couldn't keep the hungry Kilmer off the field. When the Saints opened the regular season, Kilmer was the starting quarterback. On the bus ride to Tulane Stadium for the season opener, Kilmer called to Owen.

"George, how much money was that contract for?" said Kilmer, who was told it was for $27,500 annually.

Cuozzo was traded to Minnesota a year later. And Kilmer would become a fixture before being traded to Washington after the 1970 season. In Washington, he eventually beat out Sonny Jurgenson for the starting spot and led the Redskins to five playoff appearances in seven seasons.

"Billy was a strong and very emotional leader," guard Jake Kupp said. "They criticized him that he couldn't throw a spiral, but he really got the job done. Gary had great technique. Billy had that emotional leadership. And with the type of team we had, we needed that emotion and that toughness that he brought to the team."

Known as "Furnace Face" for his ruddy cheeks and fondness for bottle-tipping, Kilmer had a knack for making plays, but his numbers never took off until he was dealt to Washington.

"You knew when Kilmer was in the game something was going to happen," said Ray Rissmiller, a starting tackle in '67. "And it wasn't always good.

"Kilmer threw what we called an option pass. You had an option to catch it at either end. He couldn't throw a spiral at all. But he was our guy. He was a heck of a leader."

Steve Stonebreaker

Before there was Kyle Turley, there was Steve Stonebreaker, perhaps the most aptly named Saint ever.

Stonebreaker was a hulk of a man, a rock-solid 6-3, 230. He was a surprise addition through the expansion draft in 1967. Stonebreaker had suffered a severe knee injury in 1966, and the Colts assumed the Saints would see him as damaged goods and pass over him in the draft.

In fact, Stonebreaker was so shocked and upset when the Saints selected him that he threatened to retire. He had started a bustling insurance business in Baltimore and his five kids were rooted in school there. Eventually though, Stonebreaker relented and joined the Saints.

"Stoney" made his presence felt at the first practice. A rookie cornerback made the critical error of failing to alert Stonebreaker of an on-coming "crack-back" block which blind-sided the veteran linebacker.

"Come here, rookie!" Stonebreaker barked on his way back to the huddle. "You see these legs? Well, they're supporting five kids. The next time that flanker's in position to block, I expect a signal!"

The cornerback sheepishly replied, "Yes, sir, Mr. Stonebreaker."

In that moment, a team enforcer had emerged.

Play Brawl

In the fourth game of the 1967 season, Stonebreaker let the entire National Football League know that while the Saints were an expansion team they would not be pushovers.

On the penultimate play of a 27-21 loss to the New York Giants at Yankee Stadium, Tom Hall snared a 17-yard pass from Gary Cuozzo near midfield and ran out of bounds in front of the Giants bench with five seconds to play. Hall collided with Giants center Gregg Larson, who was standing five yards deep on the sideline.

Thinking his teammate had suffered a cheap shot, Stonebreaker sprinted across the field and threatened Larson. The officials sent Stonebreaker to the bench so they could run the game's final play.

Atkins sat next to Stonebreaker on the bench.

"He said, 'I'm going to get that guy after the game. You with me?'" Atkins said. "I was worn out, but I couldn't say, no. I said, 'Yeah.'

"After the game was over with [Stonebreaker] said, 'Doug, just follow me.' Nobody else knew what we were doing. We were on our own. And, buddy, he took off over there and he found [Larson]."

Stonebreaker blind-sided the unsuspecting Larson and the melee ensued.

"Stoney and I were the only ones over there for a while and they were just working on us," Atkins said. "We were in the hornets' nest.

"I swatted one (Giants player) this way, and one that way. I think we fought all the way from the 20-yard line down to the 30. At the end of it, I was so tired I didn't know what happened to Stonebreaker. About three or four of them had a hold of me. I was so weak I couldn't hold them up. I couldn't pick my arms up. I was at their mercy. Some old defensive halfback for them was standing about five or six feet from me and was just hitting me with his headgear like he was beating on a drum."

Out of the corner of Atkins's headgear he saw fellow lineman Dave Rowe racing to the rescue.

"His arms were a turning, and he hit that whole pile and knocked them all off of me," Atkins said. "I was never so glad to see a man in all my life."

The brawl spilled into the stadium exits and into the stands before police restored order. Saints color analyst Norman Van Brocklin called it "the best fight in Yankee Stadium in years."

"It was something I had to do," Stonebreaker told Pete Finney of *The States-Item* that day. "You got to figure it this way: let those guys keep taking cheap shots—and getting away with it—and there's no end to it."

Fans were so taken by Stonebreaker's courage that dozens sent him checks to help offset the fine levied to him by the NFL for starting the incident.

Stonebreaker became an instant hit in New Orleans.

A pack of loyal fans draped a huge banner over the rail in the upper deck of the south end zone bearing the title of his unofficial fan club: "Stoney's Sinners."

"Hell, I think the NFL should have awarded me a bonus for pointing out the deficiencies in sideline security," Stonebreaker later told *The Times-Picayune*.

Stonebreaker was named a public relations officer at Maison Blanche after his first season and eventually became a successful financial packager in the city. His life ended tragically in 1995 when he died from an apparent suicide at the age of 56.

CHAPTER 2

Growing Pains
(1968-1977)

J.D. Roberts

John Mecom named J.D. Roberts interim head coach after firing Tom Fears on November 2, 1970.

Roberts came to the Saints from the Richmond Roadrunners of the Continental Football League, where his team has posted a less-than-inspiring 1-7 record.

That didn't endear him to the local critics, who felt Mecom should have recognized his deficiencies and hired a proven winner. Instead, Mecom rewarded Roberts with a two-year contract in January, 1971.

Usually a new head coach benefits from a honeymoon period. No so for Roberts. On the day Roberts was hired, *States-Item* columnist Peter Finney made an ominous yet prescient prediction.

"I'd be less than honest if I told you I see hope in the future—and this is certainly no reflection on J.D. Unlike the young coach who feels the Saints 'will be winning' by the end of this contract, my reading is one of impending disaster. For the good of the franchise, let's hope I'm entirely wrong when I tell you the Saints now resemble the *Titanic* on her maiden voyage. The icebergs cometh."

J.D. Roberts's finest moment was his coaching debut. The Saints stunned Detroit 19-17 on Tom Dempsey's historic 63-yard field goal as time expired. The Saints carried Roberts off the field on their shoulders.

"They carried J.D. off the field like he was a hero," longtime *Times-Picayune* columnist Peter Finney said. "J.D. was on top of the world."

It was all downhill from there. The Saints lost their final six games of the season, and Roberts won only six of the next 34 games.

No. 32 Can Play

A rchie Manning remembers his first preseason game as a Saints quarterback under J.D. Roberts.

Manning had signed a contract only a week earlier and was not ready to play, so Roberts asked him to stick by him on the sideline to monitor the offense. The Saints were playing the Bills in Buffalo.

"I'm following him with the clipboard and O.J. (Simpson) is running all over the place," Manning said. "He was in his third year. He wasn't that well known at the time, but he still was the Heisman Trophy winner and the No. 1 overall pick in the draft."

On one of Simpson's early carries, he juked a defender and bolted downfield for a 30-yard gain.

"J.D. turns to me and says, 'I don't know who that No. 32 is, but he's a damn good-looking running back!'" Manning said. "I couldn't tell if J.D. was serious or not. That's the way J.D. was. He was hard-core marine and he kind of wanted you to think he didn't care who O.J. Simpson was. But I thought to myself, 'Here I am in the NFL and our head coach doesn't even know who O.J. Simpson is.'"

Roberts was fired during the 1973 exhibition season. His final record was 7-25-3.

Tom Dempsey

Tom Dempsey was born without toes on his right foot and a withered right arm. But he never considered himself handicapped. Dempsey refused to allow his disability to prevent him from pursuing his dreams.

In high school, Dempsey was a lineman in football and competed on the wrestling and track teams. He played defensive end at Pamona Junior College, then spent the 1968 season on the taxi squad of the San Diego Chargers.

A year later, fitted with a special football shoe, Dempsey earned a roster spot with the Saints.

On November 8, 1970, Dempsey made the most famous kick in Saints history, a 63-yard field goal to beat the Lions 19-17. The play will live forever in the lore of Saints fans and is still regarded as the greatest play in team history.

Denver's Jason Elam tied Dempsey's mark with a 63-yard field goal against Jacksonville in 1998. But no one has ever kicked one farther.

"I don't think about it every day," Dempsey says today. "I do recall something Chuck Knox (later Dempsey's coach with the Los Angeles Rams) always said. 'He who lives in the past, dies in (expletive).' It was a big time in my life. And I'm proud of it. But if that's as good as I'm ever going to get in life, they might as well shoot me."

Presidential Pardon

Tom Dempsey could have been elected Mayor of New Orleans on November 8, 1970. The night of his historic kick, he and several teammates went to the French Quarter to celebrate.

Their destination was Jimmy Moran's popular La Louisiane restaurant.

Joe Impastato, a waiter at La Louisiane, recalled that Saints tight end Dave Parks and wide receiver Danny Abramowicz had telephoned ahead so that a large table could be set up to accommodate Dempsey's celebration of his historic kick.

Unbeknownst to Dempsey, several teammates had already arrived at the restaurant and had congregated at a table in the back. Among the group were Parks, Abramowicz, Billy Kilmer, Steve Stonebreaker and Jerry Sturm.

"Dempsey walks in and he had an entourage with him," Kilmer said. "He's up in front of the restaurant and everyone starts clapping for him and congratulating him. We're all sitting back in the back and Dempsey doesn't see us."

A friend of Parks who was sitting at the back table placed a call to the front desk at the restaurant.

"David Parks and Danny called me over on the side," Impastato said, "and told me to bring a telephone over to the table and tell Tom that President Nixon was calling to congratulate him on his kick."

Impastato brought a phone to the table, plugged it in and told Dempsey that Nixon was on the other end.

"Tom is saying, 'Yes, Mr. President. Thank you, Mr. President. Yes sir, Mr. President,'" Impastato said. "Then he realizes it's one of Parks's friends, not the president and he says '(Expletive) Mr. President' and slams the phone down."

Dempsey added, "I knew right away that the president didn't have a Texas accent."

John North

John North was hired to replace J.D. Roberts on August 23, 1973, and the former marine quickly made an impression with his salty language and emotional sideline behavior.

A generally congenial sort, North could explode in an instant.

During an exhibition game against the New York Jets, North tore into free safety Doug Wyatt after a Joe Namath touchdown pass.

When North finished, Wyatt said, "But Coach, I wasn't on the field for that play."

North's fiery antics carried over to team meetings.

"He'd swear so much (tight end) John Beasley used to keep count in his notebook," defensive end Steve Baumgartner said. "He'd be flying along, 'That's five. That's ten.' Beasley could hardly keep up. 'Shit' and 'damn' didn't even count, and Beasley would still fill up a note-book."

Revolving Door

Players came and went with astonishing speed during North's tenure.

"Our dressing room looked like Grand Central Station," Archie Manning said of the 1973 preseason. "Any time a good team would cut a player, we'd pick him up.

"We were in an exhibition game at Tulane Stadium, and we get a turnover in the third quarter and jump out on the field. I'm calling the play, and all of a sudden there's a guy in the huddle I've never seen before.

"I asked him, 'Who are you?' It turned out he was a wide receiver who had signed with us the day before, but I must have missed him in practice. We went ahead and ran the play. He was probably cut the next week."

Manning said it wasn't uncommon for North to bring 120 players to training camp and then add players as the preseason progressed.

"We weren't very good, so we were always trying to find new players," Manning said. "I remember our locker room always was filled with suitcases, players coming and going."

Disastrous Debut

North's first game was a disaster of epic proportions. The archrival Falcons waxed the Saints 62-7, setting 35 franchise records along the way.

Falcons center Jeff Van Note later said, "the Saints just laid down like dogs" and "quit halfway through the first quarter."

The defeat was so bitter, safety Tommy Myers sat in his locker for an hour in full uniform before undressing.

"Coach North came in and said, 'Don't any of you ever ask to be traded again. I just put the whole bunch of you on waivers and nobody wanted any of you guys,'" Myers said. "From the back of the room somebody yelled out, 'What, even Archie?' And North said, 'Yeah, even Archie.'"

Wide receiver Danny Abramowicz took a streak of 77 consecutive games with a reception into the season opener against Atlanta.

As the final losing minutes ticked off, Abramowicz mentioned the situation to Manning on the sidelines and asked him to tell North about it.

"Archie tapped him on the shoulder and said, 'I don't know if you know about it, but Danny has a record we ought to keep going.'" North simmered, pointed at the scoreboard, then exploded. "He told Archie, 'You want a record? I'll show you a record. Look at that (expletive) scoreboard!'"

The 62-point scoring output remains the highest by an opponent in Saints history.

Mosquitoville

Under North, the Saints moved training camp from Vero Beach, Florida, to Thibodaux, Louisiana.

The summer of 1975 was particularly hot and humid. The conditions were miserable for football players; but it was a utopia for mosquitoes. The heavy rains that soaked the area just before camp provided a perfect breeding ground.

"Our standard issue of equipment was jocks, socks, T-shirt and a can of bug spray," defensive tackle Derland Moore said. "I kid you not."

Defensive end Steve Baumgartner remembers hitting the blocking sled during drills and how each collision would ignite clouds of mosquitoes.

"We had these zappers," quarterback Archie Manning said. "Maybe six or eight of them out there. You'd hear the bugs hit it. Just zap after zap. It got to the point where you couldn't even hear my cadence. You know how teams now practice with speakers for loud games? Well, we were ahead of our time. It was loud out there."

Practices were so wet and bug-infested the Saints decided to move to Tulane Stadium, busing back and forth for the final week of camp. Coach John North became so fed up with the trek that he ditched the team near the end of camp, opting to ride to Thibodaux with team athletic trainer Dean Kleinschmidt, who had brought his own car in case players suffered injuries that required hospital treatment.

"Going to New Orleans then back to Thibodaux was hard," former offensive lineman Emanuel Zanders said. "Your body wasn't prepared for that. These buses were not like the nice buses. They were city buses with that hard, hard plastic. Those would hurt your back in 15 minutes."

Hank Stram

John North was shown the door on October 27, 1975, one day after a grim 38-14 loss at the Los Angeles Rams. The Saints' 1-5 start was particularly miserable. They had been blown out by two or more touchdowns in four of the losses.

Mecom named director of pro personnel Ernie Hefferle the interim coach. In his first game, the Saints beat Atlanta, 23-7. They lost their final seven games to finish 2-12. The .143 winning percentage was the worst mark in club history.

North's final record was 11-23.

After the failures of J.D. Roberts and North, Mecom was under pressure to hire a big name. Hank Stram was the answer. Mecom announced the hiring to much fanfare on January 20, 1976.

Stram guided the Dallas Texans and Kansas City Chiefs to three AFL titles and the Super Bowl IV championship. He was hired before the 1976 season and was given the title of vice president after having spent 1975 as a television commentator. He stood only under Mecom on the club's organizational chart.

With a five-year contract in hand, Stram took a long-term approach to the rebuilding job. That long-term approach ultimately proved costly.

One thing Stram didn't plan on was not having Archie Manning, the player Stram later referred to as "a franchise player without a franchise."

"I got a call from the league after the 1975 season to invite me to play in the Pro Bowl as an injury replacement," Manning said. "I wanted to go, but I knew my shoulder wasn't right. I told them I'd call them back. I went out in the back yard with Olivia and tried to throw a few passes, but my arm was shot. I called them back and declined the invitation."

On the night before Stram was officially introduced as head coach, Manning called Stram to tell him about his shoulder. Stram immediately put Manning on a plane to see a specialist in St. Louis. He would eventually see doctors in three states.

He underwent shoulder surgery in March and again in August and missed Stram's entire first season.

"One of the biggest disappointments of my career was playing only 10 games under Hank Stram," Manning said. ". . . Such a fertile football mind."

Practice, Practice, Practice

Stram loved practice more than any other aspect of his job. He quickly caught the attention of his players when he scheduled three-a-day workouts for his first training camp in 1976.

During the first team meeting at camp, Stram sold his players on the value of extra preparation.

"Hank told us, 'When we open the season against Minnesota, we'll have had 180 practices to Minnesota's 30,'" defensive tackle Derland Moore said. "He said, 'This is my whole philosophy on being able to be competitive and perform. It takes practice, practice, practice. We should be able to whip them.'"

Moore remembers the bewildered feeling in the locker room after the Vikings crushed the Saints 40-9 in Stram's debut.

"We had an offensive tackle named Donnie Morrison, a big, old cowboy from Texas who didn't talk much," Moore said. "I'll never forget after that game, Morrison sitting there and taking off his shoulder pads and saying to no one in particular, 'I'd like to thank Coach Stram for not letting us get embarrassed today. Just think what the score would have been if we hadn't had those 180 practices. It would have been 100-9.'"

Rug Burns

One of Stram's worst-kept secrets was that he wore a toupee. He refused to be seen in public without it.

Legend has it that Stram once demanded to nurses that they not remove his hairpiece for a surgical procedure he was about to undergo.

In his first season, Stram once challenged rookie tackle Jeff Hart to a game of racquetball at the team facility in suburban Metairie.

"Jeff said, 'Yeah, I'll play with you,'" former athletic trainer Dean Kleinschmidt remembered. "Well while they're playing, Hart rips a shot that hits Stram dead at the base of the skull and knocks his toupee forward. Well, Stram brought the guy to training camp, then kept him around until the last cut before letting him go, the kiss of death for a player because all of the roster spots were taken around the league. He wanted to make sure that his story would never get out."

Chuck Muncie endured a similar experience one night in 1977. Muncie was on his way home late in the evening when he realized he had left his playbook back at the team facility. Fearing a steep fine, he returned to camp to retrieve the book to find only Stram's Lincoln Continental Mach V parked in the lot.

"I thought, 'Coach is still here. Good, I can get in,'" Muncie said. "The door was open, and I walked in and Hank was coming out of the shower. He didn't have his toupee on. I didn't know what to think. I had never seen him without it. I didn't know he was bald. My jaw dropped when I looked at him. He said, 'If you say anything I'm going to fine you $20,000!' I just turned and walked out the door."

Short Stay

S tram liked to set high goals for his teams—even if they were unreachable.

The Dallas Cowboys discovered this during their preparations for Super Bowl XII in New Orleans. Dallas held meetings and practices at the Saints facilities that week.

Cowboys players and coaches enjoyed a good laugh when they arrived for their first practice on Tuesday and read some of the signs posted in the Saints' locker room, particularly the one that began "To win the Super Bowl" and went on to list the Saints goals set forth by Stram for 1977.

Among them, the New Orleans defense was asked to cause three fumbles a game, stop all third-down plays of two or less yards and give up 14 points a game or less. The offense was expected to "never allow any sacks on the quarterback, never fumble, never throw any interceptions and score 25 points a game."

"Ridiculous, totally unrealistic," Cowboys assistant Ermal Allen said.

The death knell for Stram was the shocking 33-14 loss to Tampa Bay on December 11, 1977. It was the first win in Bucs' history and snapped a 26-game losing streak.

The writing was on the wall afterward when Mecom told reporters, "I'll be damned if I see any of the progress [Stram] always talks about."

Stram was fired a few days later.

"Maybe more was expected of Hank than some of the coaches we had around here," said former Saints general manager Harry Hulmes. "Was Hank up to making something of nothing? He won seven games in two years when maybe the very best possible record, considering the team he was working with, was eight or nine."

Stram's two-year record was a woeful 7-21.

"Hank thought he had a five-year deal, but he didn't," Manning said. "He was doing a long-term approach here and they cut it short after two years."

Chuck Muncie

A sk Chuck Muncie what he thinks of Deuce McAllister and he'll flash that kilowatt smile and shrug, "He's all right."

If McAllister isn't the most talented running back in Saints history, Muncie is. No other runners are even in the discussion.

Ricky Williams, Dalton Hilliard and George Rogers were and are great backs. But Muncie and McAllister are special.

"Chuck was one of those backs who come along every eight or 10 years," Manning said. "He could have been one of the all-time greats. He was that big and that fast."

Added Derland Moore: "Chuck could have been a Hall of Famer."

Muncie, however, never applied himself and fought a constant battle with drugs while playing four star-crossed seasons with the Saints from 1976 to 1980.

Hank Stram made Muncie the No. 3 overall pick in the 1976 draft. He followed that selection with speedy Tony Galbreath early in the second round. Stram dubbed the tandem "Thunder and Lightning."

The duo formed one of the great backfield combinations of their era. Their production helped to balance a Saints offense that previously had been reliant on

Chuck Muncie was one of the most talented players to ever wear a Saints uniform, but immaturity and a drug problem prevented him from reaching superstar status. *AP/WWP*

Manning's arm. Muncie was the focal point. In 1980, he helped the Saints post their first non-losing season by rushing for 1,198 yards, becoming the first Saints rusher to top the 1,000-yard threshold.

"I've seen a lot of talented people in my life, and Muncie, had he been dedicated and didn't have that (drug problem) in his way, probably would have the NFL records for rushing," Galbreath said. "He was 245, 250 pounds and could run a 4.4 40. That's something you just don't see much."

Chuckles the Clown

Muncie made headlines and not all of them were good: "Muncie Misses Team Plane"; "Muncie Lost—And Found"; "Muncie Says Home Vandalized."

He drove Stram to distraction with his deception, immaturity and lack of professionalism.

"Chuck was an artist at lying with a special charm," columnist Peter Finney said. "He was a smart guy and everybody liked him. You just couldn't believe anything he said back then."

There was always an excuse for missing the team charter, failing to show up for practice or falling asleep in meetings. His mother had a heart attack. The tires on his van were slashed. The hotel operator failed to give him a wakeup call. On and on it went.

He toyed with the media as effectively as he did opposing cornerbacks. Muncie once told the story of how his kindergarten teacher suggested he change the spelling of his last name, from Munsey, the form the family had been using, to Muncie, the form used by the original Muncie, a Native American of the Blackfoot tribe.

"With the help of my mother," Muncie said. "I discovered my great-great-great-grandfather was a Blackfoot Indian. And his wife was the daughter of a trapper."

The story later was found to be completely false.

"It was amazing how he performed," Manning said. "He basically slept through every meeting. Somebody was telling him what to do every day. On Sunday mornings I would coach him up. I very seldom called a play where I didn't stop and tell Muncie what he was doing. We'd break the huddle and I would just time it where I walked by him and told him exactly what he was going to do. He gained like 1,200 yards one year on one engine. I don't know what he was doing during the week but he wasn't thinking football."

Muncie still rushed for more than 804 yards a season despite his off-field issues and having to split time and carries with Galbreath.

"I could have been so much better," Muncie said. "The game was easy for me. I was a natural athlete. To this day, I'm 50 years old and I can still run a sub 5.0 40 [-yard dash]. I never got hurt. I never had surgery. I probably could have played 15 years. ... I see these guys in the Hall of Fame and I know I'm as good as those guys. I just never applied myself."

CHAPTER 3

The Struggle Continues:
Nolan to Bum
(1978-1985)

Dick Nolan

After firing Hank Stram, Mecom considered several big-name coaches, including George Allen and Don Coryell, to replace Stram. He settled on Dick Nolan, the former defensive back for the New York Giants in their glory years, and a former successful coach at San Francisco.

Nolan was hired on February 6, 1978, nine days after Stram's dismissal. Shortly thereafter, Nolan introduced his inaugural highlight film entitled "Someday Soon."

The intense and quiet Nolan earned the nickname Mute Rockne during his tenure with the San Francisco 49ers. A disciple of Tom Landry's "flex" defense, which had been used with great success by his 49ers teams and the Dallas Cowboys, Nolan set about improving the talent-shy defense.

Nolan was known for his steady demeanor and diligent work ethic.

"Dick didn't say a whole lot," former athletic trainer Dean Kleinschmidt said. "He liked to keep a low profile."

His actions spoke louder than his words. During his first two seasons, Nolan enjoyed the most success of any Saints coach in history.

His first team went 7-9 in 1978. Three of those losses were heartbreakers. Owner John Mecom rewarded Nolan with a raise and a contract extension. He also extended Manning's contract. Hope beckoned in 1979.

Nolan's second team took another step forward. Brandishing the NFL's fourth-ranked offense, the Saints posted the first non-losing season in club history and sent a record five players to the Pro Bowl.

Team officials and the long-suffering fans were so caught up in the euphoria of finally being a playoff contender that they overlooked the small signs of trouble that began to reveal themselves.

In the final exhibition game of the 1979 season, running back Chuck Muncie didn't arrive for the game until the second quarter. He told Nolan he was held up by a minor traffic accident.

The ill-fated decision to draft punter-kicker Russell Erxleben with the No. 11 pick in the first round also started to rear its ugly head. In his first game as a Saint, Erxleben was involved in the decisive play of a gutwrenching 40-34 overtime loss to archrival Atlanta. Tied at 34 in overtime, the Saints dropped back into punt formation at their own 40-yard line in the Superdome. Backup center John Watson snapped the ball over Erxleben, who fielded the ball near his goal line. Erxleben tried to throw a pass as he was hit. The chest-high pass was intercepted by Falcons running back James Mayberry at the 6, and he ran it in for the winning points.

The loss sent the Saints spiraling into a three-game losing streak to start the season. They rallied to go 8-8 and set the stage for what was expected to be a breakout season in 1980.

1-15

The Saints lost the opener 26-23 to San Francisco when Russell Erxleben missed a 34-yard field goal attempt as time expired. Ugly losses to Chicago (22-3) and Buffalo (35-26) followed.

The fragile chemistry of the team began to unravel.

Defensive end Joe Campbell was suspended without pay for repeated altercations with officials and opposing players. Coach Dick Nolan benched four offensive starters, including running backs Chuck Muncie and Tony Galbreath.

Muncie, the lone starter benched for off-field issues, had developed into a one-man disciplinary nightmare. He regularly missed practices and meetings and was habitually late to other appointments. To cover his actions, he routinely made up wild tales: car accidents, mysterious ailments, deaths in the family.

Nolan finally had had enough. After a loss to Miami that dropped the club to 0-4, Nolan traded Muncie to San Diego for a second-round draft pick.

Saints officials painted Muncie as a scapegoat, but the trade didn't prove to be the panacea. A few weeks later defensive end Joe Campbell was traded to the Rams. Running back Mike Strachan was released. More lineup changes ensued. And the losses continued to mount.

The Saints were so bad they became laughingstocks. Thousands of fans attended games with white bags on their heads and called themselves "Ain'ts" fans. After a 40-7 loss to the Cardinals, The *Times-Picayune's* Big Play graphic depicted the Saints' Xs and Os leaving the field. "The Big Play of the day?" the caption read. "Leaving the field at 2:40 p.m., mercifully putting an end to a day they will try to forget.

"Nolan unraveled so much that Dean Kleinschmidt told me he went into his office one day and Nolan had five cigarettes burning in different ash trays on his desk," columnist Peter Finney said. "He'd take a puff and put a cigarette down. He was so unconscious."

Just Say No

The 1980 Saints were beset by off-field problems. The team was sidetracked by a lack of chemistry and discipline. The biggest problem, however, was drugs.

At the time, Saints officials denied the problem existed.

"I don't think so," general manager Steve Rosenbloom told *The Times-Picayune.* "… We are doing everything in our power to monitor the situation. I don't think we have a problem here."

It all came out a few years later in an explosive story in *Sports Illustrated*, authored by former Saints lineman Don Reese. The article detailed the drug problem that had infected pro football and American culture and eventually led the NFL to establish a strict substance abuse policy that today is regarded as the best in sports.

"It's no secret that we had a drug problem among the young kids," running back Tony Galbreath said. "[Drugs] don't match with football. I think we could have been a great football team, but the problems outside of the game threw us off. We had some athletes who had problems."

In the late '70s and early '80s, cocaine became the drug of choice in American culture. Muncie remembers free-basing cocaine during training camp in Vero Beach with Reese when the straight-laced Manning popped in.

"Don had this little stove in his room that he used to prepare [cocaine]," Muncie said. "Archie comes by and says, 'Hey, you guys cooking up some soul food?' We were like, 'Uh yeah, Archie. That's what we're doing.'"

Muncie earned his first Pro Bowl berth in 1979 but didn't handle success well. He lost control of his life and was traded to San Diego for a second-round draft pick during the 1980 season.

Muncie learned of the deal when he walked off the return flight from a road game and was greeted by Chargers assistant general manager Tank Younger at New Orleans International Airport.

"I told him, 'So long. You've been traded,'" Nolan said.

For Muncie, it was a bittersweet moment. On one hand he was upset to have to leave his buddies and running partners in New Orleans. On the other, San Diego was 4-0 and the Saints were winless in four outings.

"That whole season in San Diego I felt sorry for those guys," Muncie said. "I was out there in San Diego having a great year and those guys were struggling. Those were my boys. People were coming to games wearing bags on their heads and booing them. Those guys were ridiculed."

After the Saints turned in a listless performance before a national television audience in an embarrassing 27-7 loss to the Rams on *Monday Night Football*, Mecom fired Nolan. He turned the reins over to veteran offensive line coach Dick Stanfel.

Mecom said one of the main reasons behind the firing was "Dick Nolan's condition. I felt we were ruining the man's health."

"I remember giving Dick the injury report and looking at him and seeing the stress lines in his face were getting deeper and the dark circles around his eyes were bigger," Kleinschmidt said. "He had to rely on a lot of people for his success that had let him down."

Dick Stanfel

Dick Stanfel's first day on the job as interim head coach would be a memorable one thanks to Don Reese and Derland Moore. The pair of vocal defensive linemen tangled in a heated brawl at practice.

Before he fought with Moore, Reese, who didn't practice because of strained knee ligaments, had prowled the sidelines complaining to anyone who would listen.

"I want out," Reese said to reporters. "These people don't know how to win."

As Reese continued, Joe Federspiel, a linebacker, took exception and exchanged words with him.

Moore countered with a comment. Reese responded. And the shouting began.

"You quit," Moore shouted at Reese, igniting the fray, which resumed in the postpractice locker room where chairs were tossed and shirts were violently ripped.

"It was Dick's first day on the job, and what a day it was," trainer Dean Kleinschmidt said. "It was raining. No one was in a good mood. Don Reese comes in and starts talking about how some of the veterans weren't doing their job. It didn't sit well with Derland Moore. One thing led to another. Suddenly, I'm watching the kind of fight they must have had in those wild west saloons. This one in an NFL locker room—no helmets, no pads, just bare knuckles. And plenty of rage."

To this day, Moore said it was the nastiest fight of his life. And Moore was never afraid to mix it up with anyone.

"I've never punched someone harder in my life," Moore said. "I seriously wanted to kill that man. I was punching him so hard in the face his head cocked back and hit the cinder-block wall. He just got up and shook it off. You don't do that without being on something. A normal person would not have gotten up from that."

Reese, who was suspended for the final four games of the season, gave his account of the brawl in the infamous *Sports Illustrated* cover story in 1983.

"When they tried to pull us apart, I fought everybody in sight," Reese said. "They had to gang up on me to hold me down. And when they let me up, I fought all the way to the dressing room. I was hysterical. I couldn't stop fighting. I wanted to stop, but I couldn't. I don't know what I did or who I did it to, but when we got inside I jumped Moore again. At that moment I hated him. I wanted to kill him. It was my messed-up mind doing it, because I actually liked Derland Moore."

Skid Continues

The coaching change did not change the Saints' fortunes.

In Stanfel's debut as interim head coach, Minnesota edged the Saints 23-20 when Matt Blair blocked a 25-yard field goal attempt by Bennie Ricardo in the final minute. The block spoiled a furious comeback from a 23-0 deficit.

A play before the failed kick, the Saints appeared to have scored the go-ahead touchdown when Archie Manning swept into the end zone on a quarterback option to convert a third and goal from the 3-yard line.

However, officials ruled Tony Galbreath was guilty of a false start infraction. That made it third and goal from 8, and Manning's pass to Ike Harris was knocked down to set up Ricardo's failed attempt.

"I cried for Tony," Manning said. "I didn't think it could ever get any worse."

A week later, it did.

The Saints squandered the biggest lead in NFL history—a 35-7 halftime margin—in a bitter 38-35 overtime loss at San Francisco.

Nolan, wearing sunglasses, a hat and turned-up collar, watched the grim comeback from the stands.

"There's no way I thought we could lose at halftime—no way," safety Tommy Myers said. "Not with a 35-7 lead."

The 49ers were motivated by some trash talking before the second-half kickoff.

"We heard them coming down the tunnel (to start the second half) shouting, 'Let's make it 70-7,'" 49ers coach Bill Walsh said. "That didn't help."

The loss made the Saints—along with the 1977 Tampa Bay Buccaneers—only the second team in NFL history to lose 14 games in a season. Dick Stanfel finished the season with a 1-3 career mark.

Bum Phillips

The whims of John Mecom's coaching hires had gone from rising assistant prospect (Tom Fears) to unknown commodities (J.D. Roberts and John North) to big-name catch (Hank Stram) back to promising assistant (Dick Nolan). The public had grown restless. This time he needed to make a splash.

And he did. The hiring of recently fired Houston coach Bum Phillips on January 22, 1981 made national headlines.

Two days before Phillips signed a five-year contract, general manager Steve Rosenbloom and player personnel director Dick Steinberg resigned. Phillips later assumed the duties of general manager.

"I want to win now," Phillips told reporters. "That's why I'm here, [that's] what he hired me for."

He raised eyebrows, however, when he told reporters he didn't plan to hire an offensive coordinator.

"I've been that route," Phillips said. "I still don't think they are that important.'"

Phillips was an old-school coach, a disciple of legendary Texas A&M and Alabama coach Paul "Bear" Bryant. He believed in running the football and playing defense. He disdained the new computerized scouting systems the Saints used and instead kept notes with pencil and paper.

Bum Phillips's Saints teams were strong on defense, but they struggled to score points due to an antiquated offense. *Photo courtesy of the New Orleans Saints*

Regardless, Phillips's first draft was one of the most successful in club history. He snagged Heisman Trophy winner George Rogers (although he passed on Lawrence

Taylor) with the No. 1 overall pick and plucked Pitt line-backer Rickey Jackson with the second-round selection the club acquired from San Diego in the Chuck Muncie trade. In the third round, he added defensive end Frank Warren and tight end Hoby Brenner.

Phillips upgraded the talent base, but his teams struggled because of an archaic offensive system.

Phillips's first team went 4-12 and scored only 207 points. They were held to one touchdown or fewer in six games and failed to score more than two touchdowns in their first nine games. Phillips rotated three quarter-backs—Manning, Dave Wilson and Bobby Scott—and attempted more than two runs (546 attempts) for every one pass (238 attempts).

The offensive struggles continued throughout his tenure, exacerbated by ill-fated decisions to trade away some of the team's top talent: Tony Galbreath to Minnesota; Wes Chandler to San Diego; and Manning to Houston.

"The real problem was that the Saints under Bum Phillips ran the most basic offense in football, something right out of the '50s. It was a joke around the league," wrote E.M. Swift in a 1986 *Sports Illustrated* article. "... They were about as tough to read as Garfield."

Horsin' Around

Horse racing was one of Phillips's favorite pastimes. He grew up on a ranch in Texas and owned several race-horses during his coaching career.

When he wasn't talking football, Phillips's conversation often steered to his horses and how they were faring at nearby Jefferson Downs.

Once, during the 1985 training camp in Ruston, the Saints bussed to Shreveport to take a flight to Boston for an exhibition game against the Patriots. When the club was told the flight would be delayed three or four hours to make maintenance repairs, Phillips took the entire team to the races at nearby Louisiana Downs in Bossier City.

"I figured, heck, we might as well go the track and spend some time there," Phillips said.

Saints officials phoned ahead and the track rolled out the red carpet for the unexpected guests.

Phillips's fondness for horses meshed well with Tom Benson, who took control of the team in March 1985. In addition to owning the Saints, Benson also owned several horses during his initial years with the team.

"Tom was my kind of guy," Phillips said. "He was a good, honest businessman who went into horses like a business, not just for fun. He was very much into horses."

Phillips loved the horses so much that it was speculated that he traded the final choices in the 1982 draft to Washington just so he could cut out early and attend the races. The story, however, was never proven to be true and remains urban legend.

One of Phillips's favorite horses was "Never Waddle," who Phillips's son Wade sarcastically referred to as "Never Won." Saints officials used to solicit office collections to bet on Never Waddle when he would race at nearby Jefferson Downs.

"The money just disappeared because Never Waddle would never win," said former Saints public relations director Rusty Kasmiersky.

A Charming Man

Phillips's laid-back atmosphere was a welcome change from the more regimented and serious Dick Nolan days.

Phillips would fly in country and western singers to perform at pizza and beer parties for the players on Friday nights at training camp. Waylon Jennings and Harlon Howard were among the stars who performed.

"If we could have won, it would have been the greatest job ever," said defensive tackle Derland Moore. "Bum believed in having fun; hard work and hard play in that order."

Phillips knew how to lighten the mood of the room with a one-liner. He had a keen sense of humor and was quick with a joke or a jab.

After running back George Rogers failed to complete a 1.5-mile run on the opening day of the 1981 training camp, Phillips quipped: "Well, if we ever face a mile and a half to go for a first down, we'll just give the ball to someone else."

A year later, a reporter noted to Phillips about the number of players on the roster named Clark (Bruce and Kelvin) and Lewis (Marvin, Reggie and Rodney). Phillips cracked: "We now have enough Lewises and Clarks to open the Western Frontier."

One of the diversions for Saints coaches during training camp at Vero Beach, was the Dodgertown golf course. On his way to Dodgertown's first tee, Phillips was asked by a bystander, "Did anyone ever tell you you look like Bum Phillips?"

"Yeah," Bum replied. "My mama."

Hardly a Bum

Phillips was known for his generosity and kind heart. His character showed through, even in defeat. The coach once rescued a stranded motorist while en route home from a losing game with the New York Giants in 1985.

Rains from Hurricane Juan swamped the area and left Dave Lindner stranded in his car in deep water at an intersection in suburban Destrehan.

Phillips used his truck to push the other driver to higher ground, then invited him to stay overnight at his nearby home and provided the astonished guest with food, dry clothes and football chitchat until after midnight. "What else could I do? He couldn't get in or out," Phillips said.

"Regardless of what you might think of his football strategy, he's a class individual," Lindner said. "How many people would do what he did? It just blew me away."

Phillips was a father figure to many of his players. He often motivated his players through his folksy chatter. Team meetings turned into down-home lectures about life and family and American culture.

"Bum was a great guy," former Saints defensive tackle Derland Moore said. "I learned a lot from Bum. I learned about life."

Each week, Phillips sent his administrative assistant to the library to collect books on motivation and management. The desk in his office was usually piled high with reference material. He started each team meeting with a speech that included a daily affirmation or life lesson.

"No one wanted to miss Bum's talks," said longtime athletic trainer Dean Kleinschmidt. "John Hill later asked

Bum if he could tape record his speeches. He was really great at it."

Manning said the pregame pep talks often "were like pop art.

"You never knew what he was going to say."

Home Improvement

One of the first jobs for Phillips, like seemingly each of his predecessors, was to re-design the coaching offices and meeting rooms at the practice facility.

"A new staff would come in and bring in three extra coaches and they would take this store room in the back and divide the room into three offices," head athletic trainer Dean Kleinschmidt said. "Then the next coach would come in and say, 'These offices are like closets' and make it back into one room. This wall went up and down and up and down."

The renovated room soon became a running joke for veteran players and executives.

"John Paul Young, who coached the linebackers, was like a carpenter on the side," Archie Manning said. "They did all this major renovation and changed up the meeting rooms. I was in there one day in April and they asked me, 'How do you like how the work came out?' I said, 'Good. This is the way it used to look when I first got here.' It was kind of comical how that room kept changing back and forth with each coaching change."

Archie Manning

The most controversial move of Phillips's tenure was the decision to trade Manning to Houston for aging offensive tackle Leon Gray on September 17, 1983.

"I needed a tackle, and Archie can't play tackle," Phillips cracked at a press conference to announce the deal. The deal crushed Manning, who had been the cornerstone of the organization since 1971.

Manning's mug was the face of the Saints franchise. He played for five head coaches and two interim head coaches in his 12-year career from 1971 to 1983.

After the Saints selected him with the No. 2 overall pick in the 1971 draft, they basically declared him their savior. He was one of the few Saints who lived up to expectations.

Manning is the only Saints player ever to win an MVP award, which he earned from UPI and *The Sporting News* after the 1978 season. He remains the only quarterback in club history to play in the Pro Bowl.

"Archie was the toughest player I ever played with," defensive tackle Derland Moore said. "He took a lot of punishment. I saw him take a lot of hits, but he never complained and he never pointed fingers."

Manning was the victim of an almost criminal neglect for the offensive line by the club's organization. During his 12-year career, the Saints invested only eight first-, second- or third-round picks on offensive linemen. Two of the first-rounders, Royce Smith and Kurt Schumacher, were busts. As a result, Manning never had the luxury of playing behind one Pro Bowl offensive lineman during his career.

Archie Manning never played on a winning team in 11 seasons with the Saints, but he showed class and character throughout his tenure. *Photo courtesy of The New Orleans Saints*

The revolving door on the head coach's office also didn't help. Manning played under eight different offensive coordinators.

"There were some tough times," Manning said. "Long days, busted plays, 'look out' blocks. You never got used to losing. The best we ever did was 8-8. But my career was not as dreadful as people make it out to be. You don't see any scars on Archie Manning."

Actually, you do. Manning underwent several surgeries in his career, including two in 1976 to repair damage to his throwing shoulder.

"Archie was a great player, but by the time I got to the Saints he was really beat up," running back Chuck Muncie said. "I remember looking at him when he took off his shirt and he had zippers (scars) on his shoulder from the surgeries. He wanted to win so bad but he didn't have the people around him."

Speed Kills

The only reason Manning survived all those years was his incredible athleticism.

One of Manning's closest friends during his Saints career was wide receiver Danny Abramowicz, who Archie called "the best competitor I ever played with." Manning and Abramowicz were the first two inductees into the Saints Hall of Fame.

One year during training camp, Manning challenged Abramowicz to a race. It started off as a good-natured competition but quickly escalated to Olympic-scale proportions as word spread among teammates and the coaching staff.

Seemingly every player in camp had a bet on the race when the big day arrived.

"Danny was a good friend, but he was known for being so slow," Manning said. "I knew I could outrun him. Guys made a big deal out of it. I beat him. I got by him right off the bat and he tried to tackle me. I knew right away that I needed to get away from him because I knew he would tackle me."

The players had even more fun with it during the Carnac skit at the annual talent show to conclude training camp.

"The answer," Derland Moore said, "was Archie's Red Ass. The question: What does Danny Abramowicz see when running the 40?"

Quick Wit

Manning was known for his sharp wit as much as his true grit. He had a knack for breaking up the room with a one-liner.

No one knew this better than trainer Dean Kleinschmidt, who spent many a day in the training room treating Manning's various ailments.

Back-up quarterback Bobby Scott, Manning and Kleinschmidt would entertain themselves during the tedium by playing trivia, testing each other's knowledge of former Saints camp hands and their alma maters or numbers.

"Archie had an almost photographic memory," Kleinschmidt said. "He knew the most obscure players and where they went to school."

Kleinschmidt remembers one afternoon back in 1975 during the dog days of three-a-day workouts at training camp in Vero Beach, Florida, under Hank Stram. A TV reporter was in town to produce a story on treating injuries during training camp. They had been allowed into the inner sanctum of the training room to shoot footage of players being taped.

"While they were shooting the players being taped, someone asked how much athletic tape it would take to encircle the Superdome," Kleinschmidt said. "The geniuses that were sitting in there waiting to get taped said, 'You'd have to figure out the circumference of the Dome. What's the formula for circumference of a circle?'

"Someone else said, 'That's easy, it's pi r square.' About that time Archie came walking through. His hair was sticking up. He was rubbing his eyes, yawning and stretching. He said, 'No, pie are not square. Pie round. Cornbread are square.'"

The entire room fell on the floor laughing, even the trainers.

"It was so spontaneous," Kleinschmidt said. "He would just do things like that constantly just to lighten the mood. And we needed a lot of mood lightening in those days."

Trading a Legend

Throughout his tenure, Manning exuded class and character. He never marred the organization with off-field problems and dutifully served as its unofficial ambassador at speaking engagements and public appearances.

Phillips took a lot of heat for dealing Manning. Archie was the most popular player in club history. He was embedded in the community and had several lucrative endorsement deals in town. He'd won the NFL Players

Association's Byron Whizzer White award for community relations. He also was a favorite of owner John Mecom.

It didn't help that Gray survived just two seasons.

"It broke my heart to leave the Saints," Manning said. "I don't think it had anything to do with Bum disliking me. I think he had a quick-fix agenda and just wanted to win right away, with his guys."

In the end, Manning came out ahead financially. The Saints still owed him a $600,000 guaranteed salary from the contract he secretly signed with Mecom before the 1981 season. The Oilers were paying him $300,000 a year. When Houston traded him to Minnesota two years later, the Vikings agreed to pay only half of the salary. During his final season, Manning was earning paychecks from three different teams.

"It was absurd," Manning said. "[NFL commissioner Pete] Rozelle finally ruled that I had to be paid by just one team: Minnesota."

Derland Moore

Derland Moore, along with Morten Andersen, Hoby Brenner, Stan Brock, Rickey Jackson, Frank Warren and Jim Wilks, is one of seven Saints to play 13 seasons in New Orleans. Moore is the only one in the group who never played in a playoff game.

Moore, who once called himself "the losingest player in the NFL," played his final season with the New York Jets in 1986, where he finally earned a berth in the play-offs.

"It was tough," Moore said. "All that losing gets to you. Then the year after I left the Saints they made the playoffs in 1987."

Moore was an ox-strong farm boy from Oklahoma. He wasn't the greatest athlete in the world, but he was naturally strong and was an anchor in the interior line for more than a decade.

Moore teamed with Jim Wilks, Frank Warren and Bruce Clark to form one of the best lines in the NFL during the final years of his career under Bum Phillips. The Saints ranked in the top five in total defense and led the league in pass defense during the 1983 and 1984 seasons. Unfortunately, Moore played those years for Bum Phillips's offensively challenged squads that featured washed-up veterans like Ken Stabler, Richard Todd and Earl Campbell.

"We had a doggone good defense, but we never could mount an offense that could do anything," Moore said.

Good Times

Moore was a notorious partier and practical jokester. He spared no one from his pranks. Even the clergy was fair game one night in 1981 at the team's annual postseason seafood dinner at a local restaurant.

Moore was sitting at a table with teammates when a priest from Dulac, Louisiana, approached him at the table and asked if he remembered him from the previous year. Moore said he did. Then the priest asked Moore if the player sitting two tables over was rookie quarterback Dave Wilson.

The man the priest was pointing at was actually Bobby Scott, the team's veteran back-up quarterback who Wilson had been drafted to replace.

"Bobby knew his days were numbered, and he didn't like Dave Wilson because he was there to take his meal ticket," Moore said.

For an instant, Moore thought about correcting the priest. Then he recognized the possibility of a good laugh. He encouraged the priest to get an autograph from "Wilson."

"The priest came up to him real nice, and he said, 'Mr. Wilson, would you be kind enough to sign this for me?,'" Moore said. "Bobby looked at him and said, 'Father, I know you're a man of the cloth and everything, but have you ever had your ass kicked?'"

Tom Myers

Alpo-eaters.

Tommy Myers heard many insults from fans during his frustrating 10-year career with the Saints, but that one was the most memorable.

And it came from a Saints fan.

"I've got a temper," Myers said. "There are times when I want to find 'em, face 'em and fight 'em for what they say."

Myers enjoyed just one non-losing season during his tenure with the Saints. Throughout it all, he played with passion, intelligence and unquestioned toughness.

"Tommy was the kind of guy who would leave it all out on the field every game," said defensive end Steve Baumgartner. "He wasn't that big a guy (180 pounds), but he put it all the line every Sunday."

The only time Myers ever touched a fan was after a 14-0 loss to San Diego in 1977. In that contest, he played with a distended toe, a dislocated wrist and a gashed elbow. He ignored the beer dumped on him and the paper airplanes flying at his head, but finally lost his temper when "one of the drunks, just salivating and spitting beer, called me a bunch of things after the game.

"I grabbed him, threw him against the wall, wanted to beat his brains in," he said. "But a police officer told me I was being stupid, which I was."

In many ways, Myers was the defensive version of Archie Manning—a standout performer whose accomplishments were overshadowed by his team's lack of success.

Myers enjoyed a renaissance when defensive guru Dick Nolan became head coach in 1978. Myers earned the only Pro Bowl berth of his career in 1979. It remains the only time a Saints safety has ever earned a trip to the NFL's annual postseason All-Star game.

"Tommy was a great player," Archie Manning said. "He would have been a multi-time Pro Bowler if he would have played on better teams."

The serious and straight-laced Myers once was the butt of a prank by Baumgartner, the team's notorious practical jokester.

Myers asked to borrow Baumgartner's camp car between two-a-day practices and Baumgartner relented— under one condition. Myers had to return it in time for Baumgartner to make his daily beer run.

"He was gone for like an hour and a half," Baumgartner said. "When he came back there was only like 15 minutes left and I didn't have time to get my beer. I knew I had to get him back."

Baumgartner, who annually obtained a copy of the master key to every dorm room door at Dodgertown, took advantage. He bribed one of the young equipment men to steal the mattresses off Myers's bed while the team was on the road for an exhibition game at Chicago.

"I gave him $20 and told him, 'Just make sure there aren't any mattresses in Tommy Myers's room when we come back," Baumgartner said. "Well, our flight home got delayed in Atlanta. We didn't get back to Vero Beach until about 2:30 in the morning.

"Tommy played so hard he was usually hurting by the end of the game. Well, here's Tommy hobbling down the hall to his room. All he wants to do is lay down and sleep and he gets to his room and there are no mattresses. He was so pissed. He came after me right away. I told him, 'I don't know anything about it. I was on the damn airplane.'"

CHAPTER 4

Mora, Mora, Mora (1985-1996)

Tom Benson

Change was the goal for Tom Benson after he purchased controlling interest in the Saints for $70 million in June 1985.

If he wanted to change the franchise's losing ways he needed to overhaul everything about it. He changed coaches. He changed general managers. He changed most of the front office. He even tried to change the team's colors and uniforms.

Benson met with league officials at a league meeting in October to discuss changing the colors, which would have been an unprecedented move at the time. The leading candidate was a blue-and-gold color scheme.

Benson backed off the idea after a poll of 1,127 fans, conducted by *The Times-Picayune* and *States-Item*, showed there wasn't enough support for a change.

Instead, Benson tweaked the uniform scheme. The changes included gold pants instead of white ones and scaled-down jerseys with a gold Louisiana logo on the arm sleeve.

"This is just part of the whole new Saints," Benson said prior to a screening of the team's 1986 yearbook film *The 1986 Saints: A Look Ahead.* "It's making the players feel like they [belong] to a whole new team, too."

Boogie Nights

By all accounts, Benson is a brilliant numbers man. He built a financial empire with dealings in banking (seven banks), auto dealerships (24 in Louisiana and Texas), and real estate holdings.

So you'd think he could read a scoreboard clock. Yet, part of his legacy will be attributed to a misread of the Superdome clock while his team was on its way to a 38-7 rout of Tampa Bay on October 19, 1986.

By the time Benson left his luxury suite and made his way to the field, the Saints led 31-7 with six minutes to play. Benson thought there were only two minutes left and began to party. He congratulated players and coaches. He waved to the fans. And finally he danced a celebratory jig.

Saints coach Jim Mora, who had seen big leads evaporate before, wasn't amused.

Regardless, "The Benson Boogie" was born.

"A guy took my picture dancing on the sidelines and it got in the paper," Benson said. "That started the whole thing."

Benson boogied again in wins against the 49ers and the Rams. During the latter, the Saints clung to a precarious 6-0 lead and still were trying to defend breakaway running back Eric Dickerson, who Mora called "a touchdown waiting to happen."

The highlight film of that season shows Benson wrapping a premature congratulatory arm around his head coach and catching a "the game ain't over 'til it's over" poke in the ribs.

"We're fighting our butts off, hanging in there hoping to hold them off, and all of a sudden Tom comes up to me on the sideline and grabs me and goes, 'Hey, Jim! Congratulations! Way to go!'" Mora said. "He was killing my neck. I said, 'Tom, it ain't over yet! It ain't over!'"

Benson didn't let the admonishment dull his enthusiasm. He became the team's head cheerleader, punctuating each home win by boogieing under a parasol on the sidelines.

As the wins mounted, fans started bringing "Do The Benson Boogie" signs to home games. The Benson Boogie became a staple of Saints home wins for the rest of his tenure.

"That started with a lot of enthusiasm, something between me and the fans," Benson said. "I've just done it when we've won at home. But I've told friends that if we win the Super Bowl, you'll see me out there."

Jim Finks

All Saints Day, November 1, 1966 was the official birth of the Saints franchise in the National Football League. January 14, 1986 was the club's unofficial birth.

On that historic day, Tom Benson made the best move of his life and hired Jim Finks as general manager. The Saints finally had a big-time general manager. They'd finally become a bona fide franchise with a credible football man in charge.

The Salem, Illinois native came to the Saints with a 20-year track record as a general manager in Minnesota and Chicago. He hired Bud Grant in Minnesota and drafted Walter Payton in Chicago. Under his guidance, both teams eventually earned trips to the Super Bowl.

"He truly was head and shoulders above any other administrator the organization has ever had," athletic trainer Dean Kleinschmidt said. "He had a pedigree that gave him instant credibility."

The first step Finks took was to land Jim Mora as head coach two weeks after he was hired. He won a recruiting battle against Philadelphia for Mora's services. That wasn't an easy task. Mora's Medford, N.J. home was only 35 minutes from Veterans Stadium. *The Philadelphia Inquirer* even reported that Mora and Eagles owner Norman Braman had reached an oral agreement to take the job.

Mora, though, had been won over by Finks's enthusiasm, intelligence and passion. Finks convinced Mora that New Orleans, despite being the only franchise never to have posted a winning season, was his best opportunity.

"I'd never met him until I interviewed, but I knew quickly that he was the kind of guy that I wanted to work for," Mora said. "He convinced me there was some potential there, that it would be special to go somewhere and win where they haven't been successful before. Jim Finks was a big, big reason I came here."

One of Finks's favorite sayings was, "I always believe you win, and then you get good."

It didn't take Finks and Mora long to win. In their second season, they helped break the spell of futility with a 12-3 mark and a first ever playoff berth. *The Sporting News* named Finks the NFL Executive of the Year. The next three seasons ended with 10-6, 9-7 and 8-8 records, setting the stage for the Saints' first NFC West Division championship in 1991 with an 11-5 record. The Saints followed that with a 12-4 mark in 1992, giving the club a remarkable 69-44 mark under Finks.

"It was fun because they'd never won before," Mora said. "We came in at a good time. They had a good nucleus and we got some immediate help from the USFL. We had some good draft picks, and all of a sudden we had a good football team."

Mr. Fix It

Finks considered himself an architect of dilapidated franchises.

"Jim used to tell me, 'I'm not a storekeeper. I'm a builder. I've got to have a project to build. Once we build this thing I'll look for another challenge,'" said former director of administration Jim Miller.

Kleinschmidt said Finks wasn't happy unless he had a crisis at hand.

"When things were going well," Kleinschmidt said, "Jim could be a tough boss, because he didn't want anyone in the organization to get complacent."

Finks needed conflict. He was at his best with a problem to solve. Like the day in 1988 when running back Rueben Mayes walked out of camp.

"I thought it was a crisis," Kleinschmidt said. "I was concerned how Jim would react. So he comes to work the next morning, whistling, as if nothing happened. He was in his glory. He had something to focus on. At times of trouble, you could always depend on him being a calming influence. He was a pro's pro.

"When everything was smooth—not a ripple on the water—he was miserable."

Deal Maker

Among Finks's many strengths were his negotiating skills. He had a reputation of being tough but fair in contract talks. He rarely cut a bad deal—for the team or the player.

One of the highlights of his career came in 1989 when the neophyte agent for second-round draft pick Robert Massey requested a face-to-face negotiation with Finks. The fresh-faced Duke Law School graduate asked Finks if he minded if an ESPN camera crew documented the proceedings.

"Finks just said, 'Sure,' then hung up the phone," Kleinschmidt said. "Then he says to us, 'I can't wait to blow this guy's shirt off.'"

The kid was Drew Rosenhaus. The Massey deal was his first as an NFL agent.

"Jim knew he could strip this kid bare if he wanted to, but he was kind of restrained," Miller said.

"ESPN ran that clip for years. Here's the brash Drew Rosenhaus negotiating with the legendary Jim Finks. Jim would say a couple of things and then Drew would stand up and start his theatrics. Jim took it easy on him and was fair. Ever since then, Drew had a tremendous respect for Jim, and Jim kind of took him under his wing."

Tough Loss

The worst loss of Finks's career came off the football field. He was the leading candidate to become commissioner of the NFL at the 1989 league meetings.

He originally was the only candidate nominated by league owners but fell short of the necessary 21 votes needed to be elected on the first ballot on July 6.

NFL owners subsequently named league attorney Paul Tagliabue to the post. One of Tagliabue's first acts was to name Finks as chairman of the league's competition committee, the group charged with formulation of football-related rules and regulations.

Privately, though, Finks was crushed by the defeat. Miller blames new-guard owners for conspiring to vote Finks down.

"Finks was the odds-on favorite to get it, and if it wasn't for Jerry Jones (of Dallas), Robert Irsay (of Indianapolis) and Mike Lynn in Minnesota, he would have been commissioner."

Finks needed 21 votes but could muster only 19. Disconsolate, he returned to the hotel where his family had planned a celebratory party that night.

"He always told me, the worst thing about it was the balloons," Miller said. "I said, 'What do you mean?' He said, he had his whole family at the hotel and one of his daughters-in-law had bought balloons. He said that was the biggest disappointment, going back in that room with the balloons.

"By all measures, he should have been commissioner. And Paul Tagliabue was probably going to be one of Jim's right-hand people."

People Master

O ne of Finks's favorite sayings was, "Good management, like a good engine, is best when it's hardly noticed."

Indeed, Finks did his best work away from the spotlight. He kept his pulse on every facet of the organization. No underling was too low on the totem pole for him. He treated the assistant equipment manager the same as he did the starting quarterback.

"He's the best people person I've ever been around," Mora said. "He walked through the facility and would make a point of talking to everybody in the organization. He was friendly and had all these little sayings and remarks and nicknames for everyone. Everybody had a great deal of respect for him, but they liked him, too."

Finks had an innate ability to read and relate to people. It was almost a sixth sense. Within minutes of meeting a stranger, he could size them up and evaluate them.

Those people skills were tested daily by the high-strung Mora. Finks was a calming influence on Mora throughout their years together.

"My office was across the hall from Finks and Mora would go in there constantly," Miller said. "Mora was used to getting his way. He'd shut the door and you'd hear them hollering at each other. Then Finks would open the door and just smile. He'd bait Jim and let him take him off on a ride, but he'd always bring him back. He was really a master at handling people."

Finks's calm, steady demeanor was the perfect yin to Mora's yang.

"He'd come into my office every day, and we'd start talking and not just about football," Mora said. "He'd just pull me out of my moods. He was a very positive guy."

Together, Mora and Finks formed one of the most dynamic and successful coach-general manager duos in the NFL.

"Finks was the perfect tonic for Jim Mora," longtime Saints assistant coach Rick Venturi said. "He filled in all the gaps. Jim Finks was not the perfect guy on football decisions. He made as many bad ones as anyone else. What Jim Finks did was unify this building. He was the heart and soul of this building. This guy pulled it together. He was one of the guys. But he was the boss."

Final Days

Finks made his mark in the NFL as a keen evaluator of talent and a crafty dealmaker. He saved his best deal for last.

Just before the 1993 draft, he traded linebacker Pat Swilling to Detroit for the Lions' first- and fourth-round draft picks. With that first-rounder, the No. 8 selection overall, Finks picked left tackle Willie Roaf. With the fourth-round pick, he added fullback Lorenzo Neal. Both players would go on to multiple Pro Bowl careers.

Finks, however, didn't get to see the deal come to fruition.

Finks had become quite ill days before the draft. A bad case of bronchial pneumonia had left him with a nasty cough he couldn't shake. On the Friday before the draft, Finks made a rare request.

"He and Mora, (Bill) Kuharich and I were sitting in the room going over all these draft scenarios when he said, 'Let's knock off and go play golf,'" Miller said. "It was very unusual for him to take off business the day before the draft. I think in his mind he knew that it was the last time we were going to be together."

The foursome played a round of 18 at Metairie Country Club. The feeble Finks had to quit after 13 holes.

Finks reported to work early the next morning, made the Roaf selection and called it a day. He skipped the second day and checked into a local hospital where doctors began tests on his lung condition.

Three days later, Benson held a press conference to announce that Finks had been diagnosed with lung cancer.

Finks resigned as president and general manager on July 14, 1993. On May 14 of the following year, Finks passed away at his Metairie home. He was 66.

"I can't say enough good things about Jim Finks," Mora said. "I've been fortunate to work for some great people in my life, and he was just a very special person."

Jim Mora

It would have been easy to question the hiring of Jim Mora. After all, he'd never been a head coach in the NFL before. The extent of his NFL resume consisted of five years as a defensive assistant in Seattle and New England from 1978 to 1982. Moreover, the eight-man coaching staff he brought with him from the USFL had zero experience in the NFL.

But unlike previous Saints hires, Mora had a golden reputation in coaching circles. He was courted heavily by the St. Louis Cardinals and Philadelphia Eagles before taking the Saints job.

Owner Tom Benson, center, hit pay dirt when he hired
general manager Jim Finks, left, and coach Jim Mora in
1986. *Ellis Lucia/The Times-Picayune*

"What do I think of Jim Mora?" former Stanford
coach John Ralston said. "I think he has the executive ability to run General Motors. He's highly intelligent, disciplined, with a great grasp of what it takes to succeed."

Indeed, that organizational ability was what impressed
Finks about Mora and made him an easy choice over
Richie Petitbon, Dick Coury and incumbent interim head
coach Wade Phillips.

The Philadelphia Stars had hired Mora as an 11th-
hour replacement for George Perles, who had resigned for
a job at Michigan State. In 13 days, Mora compiled a playbook and hired a coaching staff. The Stars went 16-4 that
season and lost in the championship game.

"He's no messiah and I'm sure as hell not," Finks said
at Mora's January 28 introductory press conference. "But
he knows what it takes."

Setting the Tone

Bobby Hebert thought someone was going to die. And there was a good chance he might be that someone.

New Saints coach Jim Mora was running his first squad through a series of suicidal postpractice sprints at their first training camp in steamy Hammond, Louisiana, and the maniac wouldn't let up.

Players were falling out like the Bataan Death March. On one side, Steve Korte was vomiting his guts out. On the other, John Tice had fallen to the field in convulsions.

Hebert was losing 15 pounds of body weight in practice alone. Now this?

"I'd never seen anything like that before," Hebert said. "If I wasn't getting paid, I would have quit."

Mora, a merciless task-master with a marine background, was setting the tone for his first Saints team. The unrelenting sun and suffocating humidity pushed the heat index into triple digits daily. Still, Mora refused to back off.

He was on a mission. His first team would be tough. They would be disciplined. And they would pay attention to detail no matter the circumstances.

That is, of course, if they could still stand upright by the first game.

Athletic trainer Dean Kleinschmidt, who was administering a record number of IVs daily, called the training camp "a reign of terror."

"I had never trained a team in that kind of heat before," Mora said. "I was going to make an impression. I pushed the living hell out of them. The big guys were dying out there on us. They were just exhausted. I never really noticed. I walked into the training room and it looked like a M.A.S.H. unit. I was lucky we didn't lose someone."

Lighting the Spark

Every coach has a make-or-break moment with his team, a crossroads where the club either follows his lead and goes forward or abandons him and falls apart.

For Mora, that moment occurred in the numbing first few minutes of yet another close Saints loss to the archrival 49ers. The 24-22 setback on October 25, 1987 would prove to be a watershed moment in Saints history.

After the loss, which dropped the Saints to 3-3, Mora lit into his team in the postgame locker room. He continued his rant at the postgame press conference.

"The Saints ain't good enough," he said. "It's that simple."

Care to elaborate?

"We're close and close don't mean shit," he said. "I'm tired of coming close and we're gonna work our butts off 'til we ain't close any more. … I'm sick of coulda, woulda, shoulda, coming close."

The now famous "coulda, would, shoulda" speech lit a fire under the players.

The Saints didn't lose another game in the regular season. They reeled off a club-record nine wins to finish 12-3 and post a first ever winning season. The city of New Orleans was drunk with giddiness. Each Sunday was like Mardi Gras.

"I don't think 'coulda, woulda, shoulda' had anything to do with us winning nine games," Mora said. "I was just really upset afterwards, like we felt OK that we had come close. I just reacted. I wasn't trying to motivate anyone. It was just how I felt at the time."

Jim Mora lit a fire under his second Saints team with the famous "coulda, woulda, shoulda" speech after a 24-22 loss to San Francisco. *Photo courtesy of The New Orleans Saints*

Looking Back

Jim Mora was named the NFL Coach of the Year in 1987 for doing what nine previous coaches in 19 different seasons failed to do in New Orleans. He won. The Saints' 12-3 record was their first ever winning season. His next six teams combined for five winning seasons and a 58-38 record. From 1987 to 1990, his teams won 13 consecutive games against AFC opponents.

Mora inherited a team that was more talented than he anticipated when he took command. The roster was loaded with good football players and solid pros like tackle Stan Brock, cornerback Dave Waymer, tight end Hoby Brenner, center Joel Hilgenberg, defensive end James "Jumpy" Geathers, guard Steve Korte, nose tackle Tony Elliott, defensive end Frank Warren and defensive tackle Jim Wilks.

"I did not appreciate how good we were, because we were really good," Mora said. "We had some really, really good teams."

Mora's Saints teams had the misfortune of bad timing. They just happened to be playing in the same division as the San Francisco 49ers, who at the time were really, really great.

"There were two years that we won 12 games, and we were a wild-card team because the 49ers won 14 games," Mora said. "Two years we won 12 games and couldn't even win a dang division title. At the time I was disappointed, but I didn't appreciate how tough it was to win 12 games at that point. It was tough."

Sudden Goodbye

Mora couldn't take another minute. He couldn't stand to coach one more day or stomach one more bitter loss.

The frustration had been building for weeks. It all came to a head after a 19-7 loss at Carolina on October 20, 1996 dropped the Saints to 2-6. Mora erupted. He tore into his coaches during a profanity-laced tirade during his postgame press conference.

"It was [an awful] performance by our football team," he said. "We should be totally embarrassed, totally ashamed."

He punctuated his postgame tirade by repeating the mantra "We sucked!" several times. He then kicked the door of the visiting coach's office hard with his right foot and disappeared inside.

That night, Mora called Benson and resigned.

"I thought they'd be better off without me, and I thought I'd be better off without them," Mora said. "And not that I had any problem with anybody there. Tom Benson was great to me the whole time that I was there, absolutely fabulous. I had a great situation there. But I burned out. And there was a lot of things going on with my life at the time and with the team.

"My intensity level was such that at that time, I took things personal. There was just a lot going on. And I regret what I did. But under exactly the same situation I'd probably do it again. I was kind of an emotional wreck at that point. And I admit it. I couldn't go another week, another day. And I quit. I quit on my organization. I quit on the team in the middle of the season. I feel bad about it, really bad about it."

Mora's final record in 10-plus seasons: 93-78.

The Dome Patrol

It all seemed so familiar. For a brief moment at Honolulu's Aloha Stadium that February afternoon in 1993 it seemed like old times for the Saints' famed starting linebacker corps.

For the first time in the history of the NFL Pro Bowl, an entire group of linebackers from one team played together, the crowning achievement for four men who grew together for seven years and emerged as the best set of linebackers in professional football.

Starting linebackers Rickey Jackson (57), Pat Swilling (56), Sam Mills (51, behind Swilling) and Vaughan Johnson (53) were the catalysts during the team's playoff runs in the late '80s and early '90s. *The Times-Picayune*

"We made sure it happened that we were all on the field together," Saints linebacker Sam Mills recalled.

They were known as The Dome Patrol: Mills, Rickey Jackson, Vaughan Johnson and Pat Swilling. And before they parted ways in the early '90s, they became the most dominant unit in the NFL.

In their time, Chicago's Mike Singletary, Wilber Marshall and Otis Wilson and the New York Giants' Lawrence Taylor, Harry Carson, Pepper Johnson, and Carl Banks were considered the best linebacker corps in the league. The Dome Patrol eventually surpassed those units in production, honors and notoriety.

They formed the core of a defense that fueled the most successful run in club history. They spearheaded a unit that led the NFL in fewest points allowed in 1991 and 1992, and was second in fewest yards allowed in the same period.

"They were the best I've ever been around," Mora said. "That was just a special group. For a couple of years there, people could not run the ball on our defense."

Sam Mills

Jim Mora remembers Sam Mills's first NFL practice. A week into the 1986 training camp, the Saints had signed the squatty middle linebacker along with two other free agents from the defunct United States Football League.

Mills had captained Mora's championship defenses with the Philadelphia/Baltimore Stars in the USFL, but even the coach wasn't sure how the diminutive linebacker would fare in the NFL. After all, Mills played college ball at tiny Montclair (N.J.) State and had been cut by the

Toronto Argonauts and the Cleveland Browns before he crashed pro ball with three years as an All-USFL star.

"When I started talking about Sam, I'm talking about a 5-9 and a quarter linebacker, and Jim Finks wasn't real fired up about it," Mora said. "I had to convince him that Sam could play."

He added, "The players didn't like me anyway, they already thought I was crazy. Now I bring in Sam Mills, and I thought, 'Oh, God, what are they going to think of me now. This dumb coach from the USFL bringing in this little short guy.'"

Mora will never forget the sight of the 5-9 Mills stepping into the defensive huddle for the very first time, looking up at his towering defensive linemates and calling the play during a nine-on-seven running drill.

"He looked short," Mora said. "He's standing there next to Jumpy (Geathers) and looking up at everyone and I thought, 'Oh, crap.' The first play he steps up and stuffs the fullback and makes the play. Three straight times he steps in there and knocks the crap out of him and makes the play. From then on, he never looked short again."

Mills signed with the Saints as a free agent. He received offers from Chicago and Minnesota but elected to follow his former coach to New Orleans.

Mills made more than 100 tackles in eight of his 12 NFL seasons. He finished with a total of 1,319, with 20.5 sacks and 11 interceptions, four for touchdowns. In that span, he earned five Pro Bowl berths.

Today, Mora calls Mills "the best player I ever coached."

"From a coaching standpoint, he was everything you looked for in a player," Mora said. "Work ethic. Preparation, leadership, intelligence, ability, everything—Sam Mills was the best I've ever been around.

"People always thought because he was only 5-9 and a quarter, that he was an overachiever. Sam had a lot of ability. He wasn't an overachiever. But he achieved as close to his potential as any player I've ever been around. I've been around a lot of good players, great players. But Sam was the very, very best."

Pat Swilling

For a dazzling five-year run from 1987 to 1991, Pat Swilling was the most dominant pass rusher in the NFL.

The whippet-quick 6-3, 240-pounder led the Saints in sacks in each of those seasons. His 62 sacks over that span were the most in the league, two more than Giants Hall of Famer Lawrence Taylor.

"Pat was a gifted player," Mora said. "He was very quick off the edge. He didn't play the run that well, but he could really rush."

Swilling was part of the fabled draft class of 1987. A third-round draft pick from Georgia Tech, he joined classmates Jim Dombrowski, Dalton Hilliard and Rueben Mayes to form the foundation of the Finks-Mora regime.

In 1991, he was named the NFL Defensive Player of the Year after registering a team-record and league-leading 17 sacks. He signed a $5.4 million contract after the season, but an ego clash with management helped ease his exit after signing. Protracted contract holdouts in 1989 and 1990 didn't help matters. In 1993, Fink unceremoniously traded him to Detroit for a pair of draft choices.

"I think success got to Pat," Mora said. "I don't think he handled success very well. Pat Swilling wasn't as team-oriented as he should have been. That is what bothered me about Pat. I think he got too selfish."

Rickey Jackson

Rickey Jackson knew what he had to do.

"I've got to make a big play, I've got to make a big play, I've got to make a big play," Jackson said aloud, as the Superdome crowd roared.

The Saints were trying to stave off a frantic comeback by archrival San Francisco on this November afternoon in 1991. They led 10-3 with four minutes left, but the 49ers were threatening at the 17-yard line.

Jackson delivered, running down a counter run from behind and forcing a fumble by Harry Sydney on the 15 that was recovered by the Saints.

"The key was I was hustling to the ball," Jackson said. "When he tried to turn it upfield, I was there."

It was vintage Jackson. Hustling. Playing his assignment. And delivering in the clutch.

In 13 seasons as a Saint, Jackson was selected to the Pro Bowl six times. He recovered 26 fumbles and had 123 sacks. At the time both totals ranked among the top five in NFL history.

Moreover, Jackson never missed a game because of a football-related injury. In fact, he played his last seven years with a plate in his face to protect a broken cheekbone.

"He was one of the toughest men I ever met," former Saints quarterback Bobby Hebert said. "I think Rickey could have played without shoulder pads."

With the pick acquired from San Diego in a trade for Chuck Muncie, the Saints drafted Jackson in the second round of the 1981 draft. He quickly emerged as a team leader with his sturdy, no-nonsense work ethic and down-to-earth demeanor.

Today Jackson's No. 57 hangs from the Superdome rafters in commemoration of his brilliant career. He ranks with quarterback Archie Manning and place-kicker Morten Andersen as the greatest players to don the Saints' black-and-gold jerseys.

"Rickey was a winner," Mora said. "If I was ever cornered in an alley and I had a bunch of hoodlums coming after me and I had to pick one guy to be with me, it would be Rickey. He was just one of the toughest players ever. If I had to sum up Rickey in one word, it would be 'tough.' The man belongs in the Hall of Fame."

Vaughan Johnson

The downfall of the USFL netted the Saints more than just Sam Mills. It also garnered them offensive guard Chuck Commiskey, safety Antonio Gibson, return man Mel Gray and last, but not least, inside running mate Vaughan Johnson.

The Saints selected Johnson in the first round of the 1984 supplemental draft. Johnson was highly regarded as a senior at North Carolina State. The powerful 6-3, 240-pound run stopper starred for two seasons with the Jacksonville Bulls.

"I knew of Vaughan," Mills said, "but I didn't know that he was such a good athlete and such a good football player. I learned a lot of things from watching Vaughan. I learned a lot in man coverage watching Vaughan.

"I figured if a guy 250-something pounds could cover that good, there must be something I can learn."

Johnson teamed with Mills to form the most physical and dominant insider linebacker tandem in the league. From 1989 to 1992, he earned four consecutive Pro Bowl invitations.

"Vaughan was a talent," Mora said. "He was just a big, strong, fast guy—really a stud.

"Off the field, Vaughan was a really good guy. He had a really good nature and was always fun to be around. You had a hard time getting mad at Vaughan."

Bobby Hebert

To this day, Bobby Hebert only remembers the splitting headache.

It all started midway through the first quarter of a 1989 game at Tampa Bay. Hebert scrambled out of the pocket and was tackled by Ricky Reynolds at the Bucs' 2-yard line. A split-second later, Hebert was hit again by safety Mark Robinson.

When he finally came to, his senses and one of his front teeth were missing.

Hebert wobbled off the field. On the way to the locker room for medical treatment, a trainer held up three fingers. Hebert answered, "Thursday."

Amazingly, Hebert re-entered the game after back-up John Fourcade left the game with an injured leg.

"Oh man, I didn't know what I was doing," he said. "My equilibrium was so off when I tried to drop back, instead of going straight back I would swerve. It felt like it was a bad dream. I didn't know where I was. I think we had like four or five holding penalties because the linemen didn't want me to get hit again."

It's still fuzzy, but Hebert does recall the look on the face of his wife, Teresa, when teammates dropped him off at home that evening.

"When she saw me. ... I looked like a freaking hillbilly," Hebert said. "She said, 'You're quitting.'"

Bobby Hebert, a native of Cut Off, Louisiana, had a 49-27 record as a starter from 1985 to 1992. *Photo courtesy of The New Orleans Saints*

Teresa knew better. Her husband didn't know the meaning of the word quit.

Hebert was revered for his toughness and moxie. He wasn't the prettiest passer in the world and his passer efficiency ratings were mediocre at best. But he was a born leader who knew how to win the close games.

In seven seasons with the Saints from 1985 to 1991, he endured four knee operations, eight broken ribs, eight concussions, elbow surgery, shoulder injuries and broken teeth. None of them slowed him down.

"I'm from the country," he said, referring to his roots in tiny Cut Off, Louisiana. "I don't know any better."

Hebert quarterbacked the Saints to three of their four playoff berths after signing with the team in 1985. He had spent the previous three seasons starring with the USFL's Michigan Panthers/Oakland Invaders.

The Saints were one of three NFL teams to pursue Hebert, a former Northwestern State standout for Coach A.L. Williams.

The Oakland Raiders and Seattle Seahawks came after him hard after the USFL folded. Hebert was poised to sign a lucrative deal with the Seahawks before gubernatorial intervention took hold.

"I already had a house picked out in Seattle, when Gov. [Edwin] Edwards called me and said, 'Hey, coonass, what you doin'?' He broke the ice right then. He told me not to sign with Seattle, that we're going to work something out with the Saints. We're going to get your agent with Mr. Benson and get a deal done.

"They picked me up in Mr. Benson's Lear jet and flew me to San Antonio and we signed the contract in a car dealership in San Antonio, Texas. I thought, only in Louisiana would this happen."

Throughout his Saints career, the club kept bringing in quarterbacks to beat him out and Hebert just continued to win the job. Before signing a monster deal with arch rival Atlanta in 1993, Hebert fashioned a 49-27 record as a starter, the highest winning percentage in club history.

"In my opinion, Bobby was a very underrated quarterback in the NFL," Mora said. "He was another tough guy and a real leader. He was well-liked by the team and respected by the coaching staff.

"I was a stickler for players being on time, and I knew once Bobby got there that everybody was there. He was never late, but he was always the last one to arrive. I think it was just his laid-back Cajun attitude."

Morten Andersen

Jim Finks wasn't one to lavish praise on a player, but even he stood in awe of Morten Andersen.

"Best I've ever seen," Finks said. "Amazing. Thrives on pressure. Everything you look for. Just the best I've ever been associated with."

Without question the greatest fourth-round draft pick in club history, Andersen arrived in New Orleans with little fanfare. The native of Struer, Denmark, was considered the best kicker in the 1982 NFL draft after a stellar career at Michigan State, but Saints fans were skeptical of heralded kickers after the disastrous career of former wonder leg, Russell Erxleben.

Andersen proved to be everything Erxleben was supposed to be—and more. Powered by a howitzer of a left leg, he kicked his way into the NFL records books and became one of the Saints' primary weapons during their glory years in the late '80s and early '90s. Andersen was

Morten Andersen's clutch kicking and powerful left leg made him one of the most popular players in club history. *Photo courtesy of The New Orleans Saints*

almost automatic from inside 50 yards and forced enemy offenses to go 80 yards against the stout Saints defense with his deep kickoffs for touchbacks.

"Morten takes great pride in his kicks," said former Saints quarterback Bobby Hebert, one of Andersen's closest friends. "He's unbelievable on game-winning kicks. I never felt more confident about a kicker than I did Morten."

The decision to release Andersen just before the opening of the 1995 training camp was one of the most controversial and criticized moves in club history.

Former director of business administration Jim Miller said the club was cash-strapped and made a decision to cut one of three players for cap purposes: Andersen, offensive lineman Chris Port or defensive lineman Robert "Pig" Goff. After a lengthy meeting, the Saints' braintrust decided that a kicker, even one as talented as Andersen, was more expendable.

"Keep in mind, the last two years Morten Andersen hadn't kicked very well," Miller said, "His line was going down. We saw him as a declining player."

Andersen was not only the leading scorer in club history but also an icon in the community. He was active in civic functions and one of the most popular players in club history. He released a hit song called "Take It To The Top" with punter Brian Hansen and was named one of the city's 10 most eligible bachelors by *New Orleans* magazine. He owned restaurants and posed for a beefcake poster that sold more than 15,000 copies.

"It was a very unpopular decision," Miller said.

The unpopular decision became a full-scale public relations disaster when the archrival Falcons signed Andersen the afternoon of his release.

In the third game of the regular season, Andersen converted four field goals, including the 21-yard game-winner, in a 27-24 overtime win against the Saints. Three months later, he set an NFL record by converting three field goals of 50-plus yards (51, 55, 55) in a 19-10 victory against the Saints. After the season, Andersen earned his seventh Pro Bowl berth.

"Our plan was to cut him and sign him back," Mora said. "The last team we thought would sign him was Altanta. They had a good kicker at the time."

Andersen continued one of the most extraordinary careers in pro football history with the Kansas City Chiefs. In a 14-year span from 1991 to 2003, he missed two field goals from inside 30 yards. He entered the 2004 season just one field goal shy of Gary Andersen's NFL record of 481.

"We made a huge mistake in letting Morten go, one of the biggest mistakes of my career," Mora said. "I always judged kickers by how they did when the game was on the line, and Morten was at his best in the clutch. He was as good as anyone who has ever kicked a football. He should and will go into the Pro Football Hall of Fame."

Stan Brock

Jim Mora unwittingly lit a spark under Stan Brock in the first weeks of his coaching tenure with the Saints.

Mora conducted strength and conditioning tests on all the players at his first mini-camp that spring. When he reviewed Brock's results he noticed a couple of deficiencies and said so in a follow-up letter to Brock. A few days later, Mora received a phone call from his star offensive lineman.

"Man, was he pissed," Mora said. "Stan was never afraid to express his feelings. He said, 'Coach, this is the first time I've ever had a coach tell me I'm not strong enough. That's wrong. I'm as strong as anyone on this team.'

"When he came back to camp and we tested him he was the strongest guy on the team. That's how Stan was. He was very strong mentally and was just the ultimate pro. He was a great leader and was very, very tough."

Brock starred for 13 seasons in New Orleans (1980 to 1992) before finishing his career in San Diego. He was a prominent member of the Saints' first winning season (1987) and first division champion (1991). He allowed one sack the entire 1990 season and was a member of a 1992 offensive line that yielded 15 sacks—a club record and the lowest total in the NFL that season.

"He was a hell of a football player," Mora said. "He was someone you could count on every day to give you his best. He was very reliable and strong as a bull."

CHAPTER 5

Da Coach
(1997-1999)

Mike Ditka

The hiring of Mike Ditka will go down as one of the most memorable and ominous days in club history. The news made national headlines and revitalized an apathetic fan base. Within a week of the announcement, team officials received more than 500 season-ticket applications, each containing multiple requests.

Ditka had so many prior commitments he didn't show up in town until later that spring. Still, his presence was everywhere. His face was plastered on "Iron Era" billboards. He appeared on TV in guest appearances on *Saturday Night Live*, *L.A. Law* and *Third Rock from the Sun*. He sang the national anthem at Cubs games. National newspapers and magazines dispatched reporters to New Orleans for feature stories.

On the local front, Ditka's hiring quieted the team's biggest critic: Buddy Diliberto. The popular WWL radio talk show host was an admitted Ditka fan. For the 1994 and 1995 seasons, he'd teamed with the ex-coach on a talk radio show from a Gulf Coast casino called *Ditka and Diliberto*. Buddy D. had spent the good part of the previous 15 months campaigning on air for the Saints to hire Ditka. He even met with Gov. Edwin Edwards to try to convince him to talk Tom Benson into hiring Ditka.

So when Ditka was finally introduced as the team's 12th head coach on January 28 1997, some Saints officials rubbed their eyes in disbelief while watching the convivial interview between Buddy D. and Benson, one of the radio host's favorite scapegoats.

"It was a no-brainer," Diliberto told *The Times-Picayune*. "The Saints were floundering, and a coach who had achieved a great deal [a Super Bowl championship after taking over the listing Chicago Bears] was there for the taking. I could sense that, for the right opportunity at the right time, Mike would be interested. It was certainly worth the shot."

Chaos Reigns

Most Saints insiders will tell you the exact moment they knew the Ditka regime was headed for disaster. It was halftime of the third game of his first season. The Saints trailed the 49ers at 3Com Park 23-0. They'd turned the ball over five times and had taken just one offensive snap in 49ers territory.

By the time Ditka reached the locker room he was a ticking time bomb. He detonated in his address to the team. Saints coaches and players said it was one of the worst blow-ups they had ever seen. Ditka flew into a rage, cursing his players and challenging their manhood individually.

Cornerback Eric Allen responded by talking back to Ditka. The coach went after Allen. Players had to separate the pair. One angry player hurled a garbage can across the room in disgust.

"I had seen him get angry before, but never like this," athletic trainer Dean Kleinschmidt said. "This went way beyond anything I had seen before. He was in a red-faced, almost-purple rage."

After the blow-up, Kleinschmidt remembers how Ditka stayed behind as the team returned to the field for the second half.

"He just slumped over on one of those bar stools," Kleinschmidt said. "He sat there for the longest time. The team doctor and I were wondering at what time do we go up to him and touch him and tell him we've got to go back on the field. Just about that time, he got up and walked to the door. But that was a glowing example of what he was trying to fight against."

No Direction

It didn't take long for Saints players and coaches to see that Ditka was navigating a rudderless ship.

Ditka liked to fly by the seat of his pants in life and he coached football in the same way. He relied on his gut feeling. Continuity and stability were foreign words.

Ditka started four different quarterbacks in his first season. Doug Nussmeier, Heath Shuler, Billy Joe Hobert and Danny Wuerffel slid up and down the depth chart as if it were a Maypole. Shuler went from starter to third string in the span of two days.

In explaining Shuler's mid-game demotion, Ditka said, "I'm so spontaneous. I'm half-berserk half the time I'm out there."

In a game against Oakland, Ditka replaced Shuler with Nussmeier, then after Nussmeier called a timeout, Ditka reinserted Shuler before Nussmeier could run a play.

The disorganization led to several bizarre scenes, none more infamous than the "Jumbo" play against Tennessee in 1999.

Leading 10-0 just before halftime, the Saints had the ball on the Titans' 1-yard line with 12 seconds to go. Ditka sent in a personnel package called "Jumbo," featuring three tight ends, tailback Ricky Williams and left guard Wally Williams as the lead blocker in the backfield. The Saints sent Ricky Williams into the middle of the line, but the Titans stopped it cold and the clock ran out amid a rain of boos from fans. The Saints eventually lost the game 24-21.

"The play before the half was absolutely the most absurd thing we could've ever done," Ditka said. "Once the call went in, we had the wrong people on the field. When the 'Jumbo' went out I knew we had no chance (to score) if we didn't make it.

"That's our fault, that's a coach's thing really," he continued. "Somebody said 'Go Jumbo' on the sidelines. Too many people were saying too many things, and that's what caused it."

No Scrooge

Beneath Ditka's gruff exterior was a soft side that made him difficult to dislike. Kind to a fault, Ditka's generosity was legendary.

CBS Sports reporter Jay Glazer had heard stories about Ditka's charitable nature before the two started to work together on *NFL Today*. Glazer witnessed the real deal off air during their years together around New York City. Ditka would routinely tip cab drivers $100. He would throw extra $20s at bartenders or bellhops.

"He'd always say, 'To me that $100 doesn't mean anything, but to that cabbie it just made his day,'" Glazer said.

Legend has it, Ditka once won $100,000 at Harrah's Casino and tipped the pit boss $20,000 of it.

"Money is not my god," Ditka used to say. "I make it, I spend it, I enjoy it. I won't die with it."

Ditka was popular on the charity circuit and would lavish unsolicited gifts on secretaries and other assistants throughout the team facility.

"I used to tell Mike all the time, 'You're too generous for your own good. You can't say no to anybody,'" said former trainer Dean Kleinschmidt. "Mike would give you the shirt off his back."

Saints defensive assistant Rick Venturi remembers when Ditka accompanied him to a speaking engagement for Venturi's father in his hometown of Peoria, Illinois.

"I was the warm-up speaker, then Mike gets up there and gives them an impassioned speech," Venturi said. "He was real emotional and had tears in his eyes. He had great presence. The whole room was in awe. Personally, he was the greatest guy in the world to me."

Bear of a Temper

One trait Ditka shared with predecessor Jim Mora and successor Jim Haslett was a fiery temper.

He squared off with players. He squared off with assistants. He squared off with reporters. He even took on the fans when the situation called for it.

In a 1999 game against Tennessee, Ditka flipped "the bird" at fans and shouted an obscenity as he left the field at halftime. The fans were booing after the Saints mismanaged the clock and failed to score after having a first down on the Tennessee 1 with 12 seconds remaining.

After the game, the Saints' fourth loss in a seven-game losing skid, a small crowd chanted at Ditka as he and the team left the field. As the coach walked past, he stopped, turned toward them, grabbed his crotch and mouthed another obscenity before walking into the locker room.

The Saints fined Ditka $20,000 for his actions.

"The biggest thing about life is the only thing you control is that moment of time you're in, that fraction of time we live in," said Ditka the day after the incidents. "And, for a moment of time, I had a chance to control it and I didn't. So I've got to make my amends and go my way and not look back because I don't live in the past. It's unfortunate, but ironically it didn't hurt anybody but me."

Hail, No!

Two weeks after his most embarrassing moment as Saints head coach, Ditka suffered his most heartbreaking loss.

Coach Ditka, lying face down, toppled like a redwood tree after the Saints lost to the expansion Browns. *AP/WWP*

The Saints had taken a 16-14 lead in a Halloween Day game against the expansion Cleveland Browns at the Superdome. Only 21 seconds remained.

The Browns, desperate and down to their last play, had the ball at their own 44-yard line. Four receivers went deep. Quarterback Tim Couch scrambled right, then lofted a high, arcing pass that a pair of Saints defenders tipped skyward near the goal line of the south end zone. The deflected ball nestled into the waiting arms of Kevin Johnson just inside the right front corner of the end zone for a miraculous touchdown and a stunning 21-16 win.

The Browns, who were 0-8 in their expansion year, streamed on to the field. Their coach sprinted to the end zone, fists pumping and screaming incredulously.

On the other sideline, Ditka toppled like a redwood tree on the Astroturf field. The front page of the next morning's *Times-Picayune* featured a classic five-column photo of a prone Ditka lying face-down on the turf.

"I was standing right behind him at the time," athletic trainer Dean Kleinschmidt said. "His full stature just buckled and he fell forward. The first thing that hit the Astroturf was his nose. I thought it was a heart attack. Then he just got up and walked across the field.

"There's no question that was the most devastating loss of his tenure."

Gamblin' Man

For a man who coached so conservatively on the field, Ditka wasn't afraid to gamble off it. In fact, there wasn't much he wouldn't wager on.

During a 13-10 win against Oakland in his first season, he lost a $25 bet to defensive coordinator Zaven Yaralian and paid him on the sideline during the final seconds of the contest. Ditka bet Yaralian that the Saints' defense would be unable to stop a crossing pattern by Oakland's Tim Brown.

Five days before his first draft in 1997, Ditka bet members of the local media $100 that Florida quarterback Danny Wuerffel would be one of the top 100 players selected. At the time, most NFL analysts projected the Heisman Trophy winner as a late-round pick, at best.

Ditka cashed in a few days later when he selected Wuerffel with the Saints' fourth-round pick, the No. 99 selection overall.

"I won," Ditka said with a knowing smirk at the post-draft press conference.

Danny Wuerffel was one of several disappointing picks in Ditka's first draft class in 1997. *Alex Brandon/The Times-Picayune*

The End

Ditka failed for many reasons.

First and foremost, the coaching staff he hired was unqualified by NFL standards. Offensive line coach/former Saints interim coach Dick Stanfel was enticed out of retirement at age 69. Danny Abramowicz was asked to make the leap from special teams coach at Chicago to offensive coordinator. Eight coaches on Ditka's staff were at least 50, including Ditka. Six were not coaching in the NFL the season before Ditka hired them.

The club's player personnel selection was equally poor. The tone was set with his first draft. In the first round of the 1997 draft, he selected Colorado offensive guard Chris Naeole, a player most scouts graded as second- or third-round talent. He followed that dubious selection with four more "reaches": safety Rob Kelly and defensive end Jared Tomich in Round 2, running back Troy Davis of Iowa State in Round 3 and quarterback Danny Wuerffel in Round 4. All four were big-name players from power college conferences. And all four were considered marginal NFL prospects by most scouts. In the end, the 1997 draft will be remembered as one of the worst in club history.

Two years later, he traded the Saints' entire 1999 draft class and two high picks in 2000 for the No. 5 selection and the right to draft Texas running back Ricky Williams. The move created headlines, but it also robbed the roster of much-needed youth and depth. Williams was injured for much of his rookie season and the Saints staggered home at 3-13.

The buzzards were circling Ditka for most of the season. To his credit, he never quit coaching or believing.

Bill Kuharich remembers Ditka calling him to his office late in the season to discuss plans to re-organize the coaching staff for next season.

"Mike said he wanted to talk to me, and he rarely did that, so I knew it was something important," Kuharich said. "He had all these plans and I said, 'Mike it's over. It's over.'

"He said, 'No, Tom will give us another year.' But I knew the only chance we had was to beat Dallas and Carolina in the last two games. And even then, it was doubtful we would make it."

The Saints upset Dallas on Christmas Eve behind new starting quarterback Jake Delhomme. But a week later they were buried by Carolina, 45-13.

Kleinschmidt said the pregame speech Ditka delivered at that game was one of his best.

"He talked about George Halas, and he talked about Walter Payton," Kleinschmidt said. "When he talked I always went to the front row. I loved listening to him—he was very motivational. He gave his speech and left the room. He and I rode up the elevator together after that and I remember telling him how great I thought his speech was. He said, 'You ought to see it from where I stand. I get a lot of blank looks. It's like I'm talking to a cinderblock wall. I don't think they get it.'"

Three days later, Saints owner Tom Benson fired Ditka, his staff and the entire football operations staff. Ditka's final record with the Saints was 15-33.

Bill Kuharich

The man most feel was responsible for hiring Ditka was then-general manager Bill Kuharich.

In the wake of Jim Mora's resignation, owner Tom Benson was close to cleaning house in the football operations. The Saints had not made the playoffs since Jim Finks had left in 1993. Kuharich knew his situation was tenuous. He needed to produce a big fish or risk being thrown out to sea.

In Ditka, Kuharich landed the biggest catch of all—a superstar coach whose name would put fannies in the seats.

Kuharich, the son of former Philadelphia Eagles coach Joel Kuharich, took a lot of heat during his four-year

tenure as general manager. He'd joined the Saints as director of player personnel in 1986 and was appointed director of football operations in 1994. He was promoted to
general manager in 1996.

Although he had the title of general manager,
Kuharich lacked the authority to wield power over Jim
Mora and Ditka. He coached on Mora's Philadelphia Stars
staff in 1983. In Mora's eyes, Kuharich was always an
underling. And Ditka was hired with the premise that he
would have final say in all football-related matters. Neither
situation was easy for Kuharich.

While Kuharich took a lot of heat for drafting Alex
Molden in 1996, nothing compared to the wrath he
endured three years later when he and Ditka made the
Ricky Williams trade.

"Billy was criticized so much for that trade, but in a
way, I think it was his finest hour," Saints media relations
director Greg Bensel said. "He was under a lot of pressure
to get that deal done. It wasn't easy."

The Ricky Deal

The nervous energy at the Saints facility the morning of
the 1999 draft was palpable.

"Everybody knew what was happening and what he
was trying to get done," Bensel said. "There was a lot of
pressure."

Indeed, Ditka had made an already difficult task nearly impossible when he told reporters at the NFL owners
meetings he would be willing to trade all six 1999 draft
picks and additional future picks to move up in the first
round and draft Williams.

Kuharich recalls coming out of a meeting that day and being swarmed by reporters and camera crews.

"I was taken by surprise," Kuharich said. "When they told me what Mike had said, I thought, 'Uh-oh.'"

Despite the pressure to close the deal, Kuharich never lost his cool as he worked the phones that draft day, Bensel said. Normally Kuharich spent draft day holed up in the war room, but on this day he never left his office.

"Billy was on the phone and he would call out to his secretary, 'Get me (Redskins general manager Charley) Casserly. Get me (Bears G.M. Mark) Hatley.' I was really taken at Kuharich's calmness. He just sat at his desk and was extremely calm and collected. He knew exactly what he was doing."

Kuharich offered the deal to each of the top four teams: Cleveland, Philadelphia, Cincinnati and Indianapolis. Each declined.

The Saints feared the Colts, who were known to crave a running back, had their eyes set on Williams. Kuharich offered Colts general manager Bill Polian the club's entire 1999 draft, first- and third-round picks in 2000, plus cornerback Alex Molden. Still, Polian nixed the deal.

At that point, people in the Saints' war room commiserated with one another, reminding each other they had done all they could.

As NFL commissioner Paul Tagliabue moved to the podium to announce Indianapolis's pick, Saints officials braced for what they believed would be bad news. Instead, the Colts selected Miami running back Edgerrin James.

"There was no doubt in my mind Indy was going to take (Williams)," Ditka said. "I wet my pants, that's how shocked I [was] that they didn't."

Benson thrust his fist in the air and shouted "Yes." Ditka jumped up from a sofa and bellowed, "Power of prayer."

Kuharich quickly phoned Casserly to sign off on a trade. The two had agreed earlier in the morning on a deal that would send the Saints' entire 1999 draft and first- and third-round draft picks to the Redskins in exchange for their No. 5 pick. The trade was contingent on Williams's still being there at No. 5 and Casserly's ability to complete a separate trade with the Chicago Bears at No. 7.

Kuharich held on one line as Casserly called Bears officials to make his deal on another line. Within minutes, Casserly came back to Kuharich with good news, paving the way for the Saints' selection of Williams.

"I was drained," Kuharich said. "People don't know how difficult it was to move up from No. 12 and still get Ricky. Turns out, Ricky would have fallen to No. 7. But we couldn't risk it. We had invested three months of research on this deal and we weren't going to risk losing him at that point."

Today, Kuharich still defends the deal.

"What people forget is that the plan to trade for Ricky was two-part," he said. "By trading away all of our draft picks, we knew we had to supplement it with free agents the next season. That's why we had $12 million in salary cap room. We planned to spend about $8 million or $9 million on free agents. People tend to forget about the second part."

Ricky Williams

Ricky Williams's bizarre, star-crossed tenure as a New Orleans Saint began on April 17, 1999. His flight arrived in New Orleans about seven hours after the Saints had made the eye-opening trade with Washington to acquire him.

A herd of reporters congregated at the gate for the locals' first interview with the new star running back.

Saints media relations director Greg Bensel tucked his head inside the plane, introduced himself to Williams, agent Leland Hardy and assorted family members, then asked the running back for a couple of favors: One, to please stand on a riser during the interview at the request of the television reporters; and two, to don a Saints cap for the interview.

"Ricky said, 'I'm not standing on any riser, and I don't want to wear that hat,'" Bensel recalled. "I was like, all right. This is a good start."

And so began Williams's short, strange life in New Orleans.

After the interview, Bensel took a limo ride with Williams and Hardy to the Windsor Court Hotel in downtown New Orleans where he was scheduled to meet with Coach Mike Ditka and offensive coordinator Danny Abramowicz in the famed Grill Room. During the ride downtown, Bensel said Williams popped in a videotape of his college highlights at the University of Texas.

"All the way, we sat there and watched it and he made comments on it," Bensel said. "It was kind of strange."

It wouldn't be the first time someone said that about an encounter with Williams.

The Madness Begins

The circus opened on Sunday. The day after Williams was drafted, he was introduced to the local media at a press conference and to fans at an autograph signing party.

Ditka stole the show at the press conference by donning a dreadlocks wig loaned to him by marketing director

Mike Ditka traded eight draft picks in the 1999 and 2000 drafts to move up in the draft and select Texas running back Ricky Williams. At the press conference introducing Williams, Ditka traded laughs with the media. *Eliot Kamenitz/The Times-Picayune*

Greg Suit. The press conference was a rather mundane affair. But the autograph session afterward was a completely different story.

An estimated crowd of 1,500 fans braved the insufferable heat for a chance to meet their new savior. Vendors hawked "We Got Ricky!" T-shirts. Rap music pulsed through the loud speakers. As Bensel and Williams arrived at a make-shift stage erected behind the team facility, fans chased after them like they were rock stars.

"It was a mass of humanity when we got here," Bensel said. "It was unbelievable."

Then Ditka took the stage and worked the crowd into a frenzy with a bold proclamation.

"I'm going to say it, and I'm going to say it loud, and I want everybody to hear it," Ditka said. "We're going to win the Super Bowl. And I'm not talking about 10 years from now either, gang. Now is the future. We got Ricky, and he's going to be the final piece in the puzzle. I really believe that."

The precedent was set. The pressure was on.

Ricky World

Williams's rookie season was a nightmare.

Injuries to his elbow, ankle and toe forced him to miss four games and part of two others. As the losses mounted, Williams's behavior spiraled downward.

He grew testy with reporters and started dodging interview requests. The rare times he did talk he was condescending or delivered one-word answers.

He showed up late for meetings and a practice. In Baltimore, he overslept and missed the bus to the stadium. The team had to send a police escort to the hotel to retrieve him. (Williams wasn't going to play in the game because of the toe injury.)

After another game, he curled up in the fetal position on the floor of his locker and fell asleep, a move that prompted *Times-Picayune* columnist John DeShazier to pen a column in which he referred to the bizarre goings-on as "Ricky World."

"What we appear to have is a confused child on our hands," wrote DeShazier.

A few months after his rookie season, Williams carpet-bombed the Saints and the city of New Orleans in a scathing *Sports Illustrated* feature story by John Ed Bradley. The March 19 story quoted Williams as saying, "New

Orleans is a great place to hang out, but it's not a great place to live and to work." Williams was also critical of the Saints, saying "I got zero help (from teammates)," and "I'd fire everyone (in the Saints organization). The secretaries. I like our trainer and our equipment manager. But some of (the other staff) will rat on you. It pisses me off so bad."

The article also detailed some of Williams's bizarre behavior. For example, Williams would throw uneaten bananas on the floor of his house for others to pick up. His room was littered with dirty clothes and sheets. He always left behind important items on trips because he wouldn't pack until five minutes before he was supposed to leave.

After watching Williams hold a press conference while seated on the locker-room floor, veteran quarterback Billy Joe Tolliver made this insightful observation.

"You know the people at Texas called him Ricky Williams. But his real name is Ricky Weirdo," he said. "That's Cliff Claven (of *Cheers* television fame) down there. He's going to go postal on us one day and come in here and kill us all. He is weird."

Headed South

As bad as Williams's first season was, it got worse when Jim Haslett took control in 2000. Haslett and Williams were polar opposites. Haslett was a high-strung, blue-collar firebrand from Pittsburgh. Williams was a laid-back Bohemian from southern California.

They were oil and vinegar from the start.

On the field, Williams enjoyed a breakout season in 2000. He became the first Saints running back in 11 years to rush for 1,000 yards, needing just 10 games to reach the milestone. On the play that reached the threshold, though,

Williams fractured his ankle and was lost for the season. He watched the club's run to the NFC West division title and a playoff win against St. Louis from the sidelines on crutches.

Williams won the respect of his teammates and the coaching staff during the 2000 season. He was tough, coachable, played hard and knew his assignments. He was one of the most diligent students on the team and would do whatever was asked between the white lines.

Off the field was a different story, however. His bizarre behavior continued.

With Ricky, it was always something. His first off season he made news with the controversial *Sports Illustrated* story. His second off season he flirted with the idea of returning to baseball. Then came the news that he suffered from a social anxiety disorder that required medication. He was arrested in Austin, Texas, after refusing to sign a ticket for a routine traffic violation. He was ticketed in Lafayette, Louisiana, for driving 126 miles an hour.

The incidents drove Saints officials crazy. When they drafted star running back Deuce McAllister in the first round of the 2001 draft, the writing was on the wall.

A year later, Randy Mueller traded Williams to Miami for a pair of first-round draft choices in the 2002 and 2003 drafts.

The deal had been in the works for weeks but when it finally arrived, Williams was taken aback and almost depressed. For the first time in his life, he wasn't wanted.

"It's tough," Williams said. "It's bittersweet for me. I really do love New Orleans. It's going to be tough to leave the city, but I'm going to a wonderful place."

La'Roi Glover

For all the grief Ditka and his regime took for their drafts, they did a remarkably successful job of finding gems on the waiver wire and in the undrafted free agent market.

None was better than defensive tackle La'Roi Glover, a 1996 fifth-round draft choice by Oakland who the Raiders waived in 1997. The Saints claimed him the next day, and the rest is history.

In a league where the size of the dog is usually more important than the size of the fight, Glover broke all the rules. The 6-2, 275-pound tasmanian devil defied physics.

Science can't explain how Glover can bull-rush 6-4, 370-pound Bears tackle James "Big Cat" Williams five yards into the backfield to sack Cade McNown. Or how he can treat 6-4, 305-pound Raiders All-Pro guard Steve Wisniewski like a silver and black rag doll.

Glover was a serviceable player during his first three seasons. He blossomed into a dominant player when the Saints signed Norman Hand to play next to him in 2000.

Glover led the NFL that year with 17 sacks, a mind-boggling number for a defensive tackle. Since the league began recording sacks as an official statistic in 1982, only one defensive tackle has sacked the quarterback more in a season—Minnesota's Keith Millard had 18 in 1989. Glover's total tied Pat Swilling's club record from 1991 and earned him the first Pro Bowl berth of his five-year career.

Two years later, though, the Saints made yet another dubious decision. They entered the off season with their Pro Bowl defensive linemen, Glover and end Joe Johnson, as unrestricted free agents. They had the cap room to sign only one. General manager Randy Mueller and Coach Jim

Haslett chose Johnson, who, along with Michael Strahan, was the most dominant end in the league.

Glover signed a multi-year contract with the Cowboys and earned Pro Bowl berths in each of his first two seasons.

The Saints spent the next two seasons trying in vain to replace him. Haslett later admitted allowing him to leave was the worst personnel decision of his tenure.

"In retrospect, it was a big mistake," defensive coordinator Rick Venturi said. "Glover was a great motor guy. Played hard. Practiced hard. But Johnson was clearly the complete player, a dominating football player. We were basically told we couldn't keep them both. The thought never occurred to us that we could lose them both."

Joe Johnson

Joe Johnson was a man's man. He had an intimidating presence about him. He rarely smiled. His eyes pierced through people. His 6-4, 270-pound frame was harder than forged steel.

Johnson was a tough guy, who, unlike Kyle Turley, didn't have to tell anyone how tough he was. One glance at him and you knew.

Johnson missed all of training camp in 1998 because of a 41-day contract holdout, returned just days before the opener at St. Louis, then stepped on the field and recorded a sack, a forced fumble and returned a fumble five yards for a touchdown in a 24-17 win.

He missed the 1999 season because of a season-ending knee injury, underwent back surgery and arthroscopic surgery on his other knee that off season and still came back to make 12 sacks and earn a berth in the Pro Bowl.

Johnson was one of the rare wise draft decisions the Saints made in the '90s. He was the 13th player overall and the fifth defensive lineman selected in the 1994 draft. He eventually would outplay the linemen taken ahead of him (Dan Wilkinson, Willie McGinest, Bryant Young, Sam Adams).

Johnson played nose tackle early in his career before switching to end permanently in 1996. He gradually blossomed into one of the league's most complete and dominant players. In a six-year period from 1995 to 2001, he recorded 49.5 sacks and earned two Pro Bowl berths. He remains the only Saints defensive end to earn multiple Pro Bowl berths.

"Joe Johnson was a great player," said longtime Saints defensive assistant Rick Venturi. "In his prime, from 1997 to 2000 he was as good as anybody in the league. He was truly a dominating player.

"He did everything well. He had great hands and played bigger than he was. He could play the run, rush the passer. And he did it with grace. It wouldn't look spectacular, but at the end of the day his numbers were tremendous."

The Saints had every intention of keeping Johnson when he became a free agent after the 2001 season. The club knew it could only afford to keep one of its high-market free agent linemen: Johnson or defensive tackle La'Roi Glover. They chose Johnson.

Johnson told Saints management he wanted to stay, but a bitter negotiation between then-general manager Randy Mueller and Johnson's agent, Roosevelt Barnes, broke down unexpectedly. The Packers slipped into the picture and stole Johnson away.

"Joe's one of my all-time favorites. He's a great guy, and he'll always be a Saint," Haslett said. "He's a heck of a football player, heck of a guy, and it's a shame that we lost him. It's just a shame, because I think Joe would have loved to retire being a Saint."

CHAPTER 6

Lie, Cheat, and Steal

Randy Mueller

Randy Mueller's tenure as general manager covered only two years, but he made an impact during his brief stint. His greatest accomplishment was changing the culture, attitude and perception of the franchise. And he did it almost overnight.

A former ballboy who worked his way up the ladder in the Seattle organization to eventually become the director of football operations, Mueller knew the value of hard work. He was a personnel man at heart. He loved to break down film of players and took an active role in scouting, even after landing the G.M. position on January 27, 2000.

Mueller's biggest hurdle in the free agent market was the stigma that was attached to the Saints franchise, a perception of an organization not committed to winning. Good players wanted to win and the word on the street was that the Saints were a dead-end. Mueller set out to eradicate that perception with a free-wheeling first month of free agency.

He opened eyes around the league by signing quarterback Jeff Blake in the first minutes of free agency, cutting a deal just after midnight and flying Blake in on a company jet for a headline-grabbing press conference the next afternoon.

He made headlines by signing a bevy of free agents with local ties: Joe Horn, Fred Thomas and Norman Hand were Mississippi natives or residents. Jake Reed and Andrew Glover played college ball at Grambling State.

He fleeced Dallas by swapping linebacker Chris Bordano—a player they thought so little of they once tried to trade him for a computer scouting system—for feisty cornerback Kevin Mathis.

He stole restricted free agent linebacker Charlie Clemons and punter Toby Gowin from St. Louis and Dallas, respectively, by offering them contracts their former teams failed to match.

Finally, he plugged holes in the secondary by signing veterans Steve Israel, Chris Oldham and Darren Perry.

When the Saints opened training camp in mid-July, they had 44 new faces on the roster and New Orleans was the buzz of the league. An organization once known for sitting on its hands during free agency had been transformed into one of the most aggressive movers and shakers in the league.

"That's a hard thing to do," general manager Mickey Loomis said. "There's a perception out there that you don't want to win, that you'll never get it turned around. You've got to give Randy a lot of credit for that. He changed the perception of this organization and that's difficult to do."

"He Treated Me Like a Son"

Mueller's aggressive worked laid the foundation for the Saints' stunning run to the NFC West division title. He was rewarded for his brilliant debut with *The Sporting News* Executive of the Year award.

Many inside the organization felt Mueller began to grow power hungry after the heady success of his first season. During the 2001 season, he exerted more control within the building and began to distance the football operations side of the building from the business side.

Mueller made his first major misstep after the 2001 season when he met with Falcons officials during the week of Super Bowl XXXVI to discuss the club's vacant general manager position. Both parties tried to keep the meeting quiet, but word leaked and Mueller was forced to address the issue with reporters.

To his credit, Mueller went through the proper channels with Benson about the meeting, but the venerable owner places a high value on employee loyalty and he couldn't have been happy that his bright young G.M. had the gall to meet with a division rival during Super Bowl week with the entire league in town.

A few weeks later, Mueller made another fateful move, turning down a contract extension from Benson, who saw the snub as another sign of disloyalty.

In what Mueller called "a bolt from the blue," Benson fired Mueller on Thursday, May 9, 2002. During a hastily called, emotional and at times confrontational press conference, Benson cited differences in "managerial style" as the reason for the firing. Two days later, he promoted Mueller's longtime friend and director of football administration, Mickey Loomis, to general manager.

To this day, Mueller's firing remains a great mystery. Benson has refused to discuss the matter other than in peripheral terms.

"I still don't know the reasons," Mueller said during the week of Super Bowl XXXVIII in Houston. "He treated me like a son up until the day he fired me."

Jim Haslett

When Randy Mueller was named general manager on January 27, a pair of assistant coaches emerged as the top candidates for the head coaching job: Pittsburgh defensive coordinator Jim Haslett and Denver offensive coordinator Gary Kubiak.

It didn't take long for Haslett to become the clear front-runner.

Haslett and Mueller were acquainted from Haslett's days with the Sacramento Surge of the old World League of American Football. Haslett was the defensive coordinator. One of the assistants on his defensive staff was Rick Mueller, Randy's younger brother.

Saints owner Tom Benson, though, had reservations. During his two-year stint as a defensive assistant on Jim Mora's Saints staffs in 1995 and 1996, Haslett earned a reputation as an emotionally charged rabble rouser who often spoke before thinking.

When Mora stepped down in the middle of the 1996 season, Haslett fired off his mouth during a meeting of football operations personnel. Benson was taken aback by Haslett's comments.

Mueller, Rick Venturi and several others, however, assuaged Benson's fears and eventually convinced the owner that the driven Haslett was the best man for the rebuilding job.

Haslett was introduced as the 13th head coach on February 3, 2000.

For Saints fans, the fiery Haslett was just what the doctor ordered. They had become the laughingstock of the league under Mike Ditka, a punching bag of a team that had lost 10 or more games in three consecutive seasons.

Everything Saints fans thought they had in "Iron Mike," they got in Haslett.

As a player, Haslett was a fiery 6-3 middle linebacker for the Buffalo Bills in the '80s. He was tough and instinctive. He once purposely stepped on the bare head of Steelers quarterback Terry Bradshaw at a game in Pittsburgh, nearly sending Three Rivers Stadium into a full-scale riot. Along with running partner Fred Smerlas, Haslett boozed and brawled his way into the hearts of blue-collar Bills fans everywhere.

As a coach, Haslett was just as aggressive. His first season was defined by bold play-calling. He ignited a come-from-behind win against Carolina with a fake punt inside his own territory. He opened the stunning, season-defining 31-24 upset of the defending Super Bowl champion Rams with a successful onsides kick. He blitzed from all angles and positions, went for it on fourth down and tried two-point conversions at the drop of a hat.

Saints fans were beside themselves. After years of passive, unimaginative play-calling, they suddenly had a team that played to win instead of trying not to lose. They were the sand kickers and not the pencil-necked kickees.

"Jim coaches with a swagger," said Saints assistant Rick Venturi, one of Haslett's closest confidants. "He doesn't coach scared. I think that's the single biggest thing that's happened emotionally to this team."

Early Challenge

Haslett faced his first major test as head coach after the Saints stumbled to a 1-3 start.

Fans were restless. They had been promised a "new and improved" Saints team, a high-powered offense and an attacking defense. So far, what they got was more of the same from the Ditka regime.

The heralded offense had scored just one touchdown in three of the four outings, all losses. The defense was struggling to make plays.

After an ugly 20-10 loss to Seattle, the Saints held an emotional players-only meeting. The offensive players wanted to see more aggressive play-calling. The defense wanted to attack with more blitzes. Haslett intruded on the gathering and quickly broke things up.

"They were saying, 'We're not doing this, we're not doing that. That we're great players and we should be winning more,'" Haslett said. "I told them, 'You're not great players. Just go out and play and let us worry about the coaching.' They were trying to test me to see what I would do."

The strategy worked. The Saints played well in their next game but lost the following to Philadelphia, 21-7. They turned things around for good after that by reeling off six consecutive wins and rolling to their second division title in club history.

Mount St. Haslett

Haslett's hair-trigger temper is notorious around the Saints complex.

Anyone who has worked for or with the fiery coach has felt his wrath at one time or another.

Saints ticket manager Mike Stanfield was one of the first victims.

It was the morning after a disappointing 31-22 home loss to Oakland in Haslett's first season. The Saints not only lost the game, they also lost quarterback Jeff Blake to a season-ending foot injury. Haslett was on a tear.

What set him off was the large contingent of Raiders fans located in the lower section of the Superdome behind

To say that Coach Haslett had a bit of a temper would be putting it lightly. *David Grunfeld/The Times-Picayune*

the north end zone. The gathering of notorious Raiders fans was so loud and unruly that the Saints offense struggled to call plays at that end of the field. The throng also did their best to throw off kicker Doug Brien during field goal and extra-point attempts.

When Stanfield arrived at work the following Monday, Haslett stormed into his office and lit into him. How could he be so stupid to sell blocks of seats in the lower bowl to opposing fans? From now on, every visiting team better receive upper deck seats or else!

From that point on, Stanfield sold only upper-deck tickets or scattered lower-bowl seats to the opposing team.

Reporters felt Haslett's wrath, as well. At various times, Haslett has confronted or challenged every person on the beat.

He lit into *Times-Picayune* beat reporter Ted Lewis and threatened "to punch in him in the face" in front of several players. Haslett was way out of line and was fortunate Lewis handled the matter with class.

Associated Press reporter Mary Foster told the Saints she planned to file a report on the incident, but Lewis did not want to make a big deal of the matter and asked her to drop it.

Still, a precedent had been set: When dealing with Haslett, treat the coach like nitroglycerin.

Haslett's favorite targets are officials. He disdains them. His detest for flag-happy referee Gerry Austin is known league-wide.

"He hates me and I hate him," Haslett once said.

One of offensive coordinator Mike McCarthy's earliest memories of Haslett came in a preseason game that Austin refereed against Philadelphia during the 2000 season.

Haslett, as usual, was on Austin's case from the start, and he didn't let up.

"He was screaming at him, 'Gerry, you're an asshole! You suck, Gerry!'" McCarthy said. "He wouldn't let up. And this went on for two or three series. I was laughing my ass off. I could hardly call plays.

"Finally, Gerry came over to the sidelines and said, 'You know I did referee the Super Bowl last year.'"

Practice Following the Rules

Early on, Haslett established himself as a notorious corner-cutter and envelope-pusher when it came to league rules. He routinely employed extra players on the practice squad. At the time, NFL rules allowed teams to keep five players on the practice or "taxi" squad each week. However, Haslett found a loophole in the process and managed to field an extra player or two at practice each week.

The practice was so common it became a running joke among reporters and team officials.

"How many players on the practice squad today, Haz? Seven or eight?" reporters would ask.

"We're actually legal today," Haslett would joke.

Talk Soup

Haslett is a well-known gossip hound. He loves to talk. The juicier the information the better. Unfortunately, this gets him in trouble more often than not. His habit of talking to the media—both local and national—has always been a bane for general managers Mueller and Loomis.

Unfortunately for reporters, Haslett is just as loose with his facts as he was his lips. His penchant for inaccuracies and false facts became such a joke with local beat reporters that they kept a "Bad Haz Stat of the Day" listing on a marker board in the media room at the team facility. The list sometimes approached double digits from Haslett's weekly Monday press conferences.

All statistics purported by Haslett during press conferences were religiously double-checked for accuracy. Invariably, Haslett's numbers were off. More than one reporter who took Haslett's word on a story was burned by it.

His embellishment was legendary. When recounting stories, Haslett routinely stretched the truth. The old saying "Never let the facts get in the way of a good story" applies perfectly to Haslett.

"He'll say anything if he thinks it helps him," said Falcons coach Jim Mora, who is good friends with Haslett from their coaching days on Mora's father's Saints staff. "He's like the Iraqi Minister of Propaganda."

Rick Venturi

Rick Venturi was the first assistant Jim Haslett hired when he took the head coaching job with the Saints. In fact, Venturi played a larger part in Haslett landing the job than most people realize.

The affable Venturi is the only person in the football operation to span the coaching tenures of Jim Mora, Mike Ditka and Jim Haslett. A great ambassador for the organization and one of the most respected defensive minds in the NFL, Venturi and his wife Cheri are embedded in the New Orleans area and hope to spend the rest of their lives here when Rick leaves the coaching profession.

How Venturi found his way to New Orleans is a story unto itself.

It sounds odd, but the best thing that happened to him was getting fired. Venturi had made the move to Baltimore with the rest of the Cleveland Browns staff in February 1996 when word came that owner Art Modell had fired head coach Bill Belichick and was on the verge of hiring Ted Marchibroda as his replacement.

The news rocked Venturi's world. Marchibroda was the one coach in the NFL who probably would not retain him, their relationship having deteriorated from a previous work relationship in Indianapolis.

Since the coaching change happened so late in the year, nearly all the open jobs had been filled. Worse, Venturi was about to enter his 15th season of NFL coaching experience, one of the magic numbers that guarantees a lucrative pension. He was sitting at his desk pondering his suspect future when the phone rang.

It was Saints head coach Jim Mora, who told Venturi he had just promoted Haslett to defensive coordinator. Was Venturi interested in Haslett's old job as linebackers coach?

For Venturi, the call was divine intervention. He said yes, knowing that his future in Baltimore was dim.

The next day, Marchibroda told Venturi he wouldn't be retained. Mora told Venturi he had an airline ticket to New Orleans with his name on it. The flight left at 4:30 p.m.

Venturi bolted from his office. He didn't have time to pack or even tell Cheri about the turn of events. Instead, he left a note on the front door of their house: "Honey, I was fired. I'm on my way to New Orleans. I'll call you when I get there."

"I didn't even have any Scotch tape," Venturi said. "I just plugged it on the door and took off. That's how this business is."

Today the note hangs in a frame on the wall of the Venturis' family room in their Destrehan home.

"We came down and fell in love with the place," Venturi said. "The staff embraced me right from the beginning."

Venturi had no way of knowing the strange twist his career had taken. Less than eight months later, Mora resigned abruptly at midseason and Venturi was appointed the interim head coach.

"Amazing," Venturi said. "Jim saved my career and reshaped it. I was just at the end of the world when he called. I'll never forget that."

CHAPTER 7

Fresh Blood

Deuce McAllister

Mike McCarthy remembers the exact moment he realized Deuce McAllister was going to be a great one.

It was McAllister's first game as a starter in the opener of the 2002 season. And this wasn't just any opener. The Saints were playing at Tampa Bay against the vaunted Buccaneers defense. Warren Sapp. Derrick Brooks. Anthony McFarland. John Lynch.

And McCarthy wasn't sure how his new starting back would handle the situation. Contrary to widespread belief, not everyone in the Saints organization was completely sold on McAllister entering the 2002 season. The Ludlow, Mississippi, native wasn't exactly the most diligent of workers in the offseason. He tended to coast and needed constant prodding from the coaching staff. Some coaches privately wondered if the club had made a mistake by dealing Ricky Williams to Miami in April.

McAllister didn't exactly quell those doubts during a listless preseason. So in the pregame locker room, McCarthy wanted to make sure McAllister knew what lay head.

"You better swell up, big guy," McCarthy said. "We're going to pound it all day. We need you."

McAllister reacted with a quizzical look. He then proceeded to blast his way onto the NFL scene with an awe-inspiring performance in a thrilling 26-20 overtime win at Raymond James Stadium.

The lackadaisical Deuce that had slogged his way through practices and exhibitions was gone. McAllister had transformed into a dominant ground force. He pounded relentlessly into the line, powering through arm tackles and slashing through Bucs defenders.

McAllister finished the day with 109 hard-earned yards on 31 leg-sapping carries. His longest carry covered 14 yards.

To put the feat into perspective, the next three weeks Jamal Lewis (17-53), Marshall Faulk (6-9) and Corey Dillon (21-59) combined for just 121 yards on 44 carries against the stingy Buc defense that would later win Super Bowl XXXVII and be compared favorably to the greatest units in league history.

"I knew right then we had a special player," McCarthy said. "I said to myself, 'I got me one here.'"

Even without his helmet, running back Deuce McAllister was so talented that the Saints could afford to trade Ricky Williams to Miami in 2002. *Eliot Kamenitz/The Times-Picayune*

McAllister finished the 2002 season with 1,388 yards on 325 carries, despite playing much of the season on a badly sprained ankle. He came back in 2003 to gain 1,641 yards on the ground and added 516 yards on a career-high 69 pass receptions.

Saints officials gush about McAllister like no other player on the roster. He is clearly the keystone of the organization, and barring an unforeseen injury, certain to go down as the best running back in Saints history.

"If he stays healthy, he'll be in the Hall of Fame one day," McCarthy said. "And I don't say that about too many people."

Gentleman Deuce

As good a player as Deuce McAllister is, he's an even better person.

Shortly after the Saints selected him in the first round of the 2001 draft, a reporter and photographer from *The Times-Picayune* visited McAllister's home in tiny Ludlow, Mississippi, to do an in-depth feature story on the team's prized new player.

The journalists made the four-hour drive from New Orleans and had a wonderful afternoon with his parents at their modest ranch house in the piney woods of rural Mississippi.

McAllister was a perfect gentleman all day. McAllister's parents raised him right. His father, a truck driver, and his mother, a social worker, instilled the values of hard work and discipline.

Even though McAllister planned to drive to Jackson that evening, he remained patient even after the visitors cajoled him into driving to Morton High School in nearby Lena for more photos.

After the seemingly endless round of shots, the photographer and writer asked McAllister for directions to Jackson, where they planned to interview two of his college coaches, Ole Miss head coach David Cutcliffe and running backs coach Rich Bisaccia. McAllister gave them detailed directions to the Jackson Country Club where Cutcliffe was speaking at an alumni function and told them to follow him.

Once they reached the familiar outskirts of Jackson, they were confident in their directions and peeled off from McAllister at a service station for fuel and snacks. As the writer and photographer walked out of the store, they noticed McAllister's car off to the side in the lot.

The reporter asked him what he was doing.

"I saw you guys turn off in my rear-view mirror and wanted to make sure you weren't lost," McAllister said.

You could count on your hand the number of NFL players who would be so conscientious. That moment, more than the awards or the yards, says all anyone needs to know about McAllister.

Joe Horn

When the Saints acquired little-known Chiefs receiver Joe Horn on March 13, 2000, fans had no idea what was coming.

Horn came out of nowhere to emerge as the Saints' best receiver since Eric Martin. Playing the enviable "X" position in Mike McCarthy's West Coast system, he averaged 85 catches, 1,222 yards and 8.5 touchdowns in his first four seasons. He earned Pro Bowl invitations in his first three seasons.

Horn's passion for the game quickly stamped him as a fan favorite. Few Saints players in history have been more revered. An earnest man of the people, he's usually the first one to sign autographs at team functions and always the last one to leave.

Horn also established a reputation as an All-Pro trash talker.

Take, for example, the rumor floating around during the 2000 season that San Francisco 49ers secondary coach Jim Mora Jr., still stinging from a November loss to the Saints, had guaranteed victory in the December 10 rematch.

"Get away from him!" Horn yelled when he saw Saints coach Jim Haslett standing next to Mora during pregame warmups. The squawking continued with a string of obscenities.

"Who's he yelling at?" Mora asked.

"You," said Haslett, grinning.

Horn is just as fearless in press conferences as he is in going over the middle of the field. Reporters respect that candidness. As a result, his locker always draws the largest crowds for postgame interviews.

But Horn's honesty sometimes lands him in hot water. Team officials have called him on the carpet more times than he can count.

After a game at Arizona, he went off on the offensive game plan and complained about his heavy blocking responsibilities.

After a game at Washington in 2003, he ripped into offensive coordinator Mike McCarthy's play-calling and called himself a "just-in-case" wide receiver.

The outbursts angered Saints officials. That both diatribes came after wins caused some to label Horn selfish and question his allegiance to the team.

Say what you will about Horn's outspokenness, but he walks the walk. In the first four years of his Saints career, he missed only one start because of injury. He played the entire 2003 season with a knee injury that would have sidelined most receivers.

"Joe can drive you crazy sometimes, but he's a warrior," Saints coach Jim Haslett said. "He plays with his heart on his sleeve. There's no questioning his heart."

Fear of Flying

The big dilemma facing Horn every postseason is whether to make the cross-Pacific flight to Hawaii. He has a serious fear of flying.

He boards an airplane only when he must and stays ground-bound throughout the offseason.

"I don't like flying at all—at all," he said. "I don't care if it's a 20-minute flight. I don't fly anywhere in the off season. The only reason I fly here [with the Saints] is because I have to. It's part of the job."

Horn made the Pro Bowl trip in 2000 only because it was his first invitation, but he couldn't fully enjoy the experience because he couldn't eliminate the thought of the return flight from his mind.

In 2001, he was selected as an alternate, but he aborted his trip in Houston when mechanical problems with the plane delayed his departure during the stopover. He rented a 15-passenger van and drove home with the 14 friends and family members who'd accompanied him on the trip.

"The mechanic came on board, like, two or three times, and it was raining. That did it," Horn said during the 2002 season. "I felt pretty bad. I may suck it up this time because a lot of my friends and family members were with me last time and they really wanted to go."

Cell-ebrate Good Times

A stylish showman, Horn's repertoire of end-zone celebrations and dances ranks among the best in the NFL. There's the Bus Stop. The Razzle Dazzle. And of course, the now infamous Cell-ebration.

When the New York Giants visited New Orleans for a December 14 game on ESPN's *Sunday Night Football,* Horn had a surprise planned.

After scoring the second of his club-record four touchdown catches in the second quarter, Horn dug out a cell phone planted under the padding on the south goal post and feigned a celebratory phone call. The sellout crowd ate it up. Horn pretended to make a call to his mother and daughter, Jhia, and son, Joseph, to let them know the show was on.

"I knew exactly what I was doing," Horn said. "I'm quite sure I'll be fined for it. For what, I don't know. I'm sure there are a lot of fans across the nation that loved that and love excitement in the game. I wasn't taunting any other football players. I wasn't trying to start fights. I was dancing. I was celebrating. Fans love that."

Saints coach Jim Haslett wasn't impressed. He admonished Horn on the sidelines before national TV cameras.

The incident overshadowed a career night for Horn. He caught a game-high nine passes for 133 yards and four scores.

The NFL fined Horn $30,000 for the stunt. A few months later, the league passed a rule that would result in ejection for players who carry extraneous foreign objects onto the field during games.

For Horn, the fine was well worth the publicity. The "Cell-ebration" was the lead story on *SportsCenter* the following day. Horn performed a 10-minute sit-down interview with anchor Dan Patrick. He did national radio interviews and was the subject of debate on sports talk shows and in Internet chat rooms across the world.

Two cell phone companies called Horn's agent, Ralph Vitolo, to offer endorsement contracts, which Horn wise-

"Can you hear me now?" Joe Horn's infamous end zone "Cell-ebration" became the subject of national debate and eventually forced a rules change in the NFL. *Eliot Kamenitz/The Times-Picayune.*

ly turned down. He eventually donated the phone to charity for a church auction.

"I won't do it again, especially with all the exposure," Horn said.

To this day, Horn refuses to reveal how he got the cell phone under the goal post or the names of his accomplices. It's suspected receiver Michael Lewis and tight end Boo Williams planted the phone under the goal post while the team waited for pregame introductions under the inflatable Saints helmet.

"I plead the fifth," he said.

For the loquacious Horn, that might be a first.

Willie Roaf

New Orleans is a big city with a small-town feel. Rumors travel quickly, and no rumor spread as fast or as widely as the Willie Roaf-Joe Horn fiasco.

During the disappointing 2001 season, a wild rumor leaked that Saints wide receiver Joe Horn was the father of Roaf's six-week-old daughter, Carrington. What started as a mid-season spark quickly spread to a brush fire. For months, the rumor had run rampant on radio talk shows, in chat rooms, barbershops and supermarkets. Some even speculated that locker-room tension over the situation contributed to the Saints' disappointing 7-9 season.

The speculation became so widespread that Roaf finally called *Times-Picayune* reporter Brian Allee-Walsh in January to publicly clear the air.

"I've talked to Joe Horn about it, and Joe said he didn't know Michelle, and Michelle said she didn't know Joe," Roaf told Allee-Walsh. "The baby looks like me—long feet, long hands; she's a big girl. But I did take a blood test.

We had it done a couple of weeks ago, so I'll find out the results shortly. But I feel comfortable the child is mine."

The next day, Horn called to dispel the rumors as well.

Allee-Walsh said he'd never experienced such a sordid story in his near-20-year tenure on the Saints beat.

Then, three weeks later, Roaf dropped a bombshell. Citing unspecified irreconcilable differences with Haslett, he demanded to be traded or released.

"It would be very difficult at this stage to repair the differences I have with Coach Haslett," Roaf told Allee-Walsh. "Things were said between Coach and myself that I don't want to talk about."

Roaf's comments stung Haslett. He respected Roaf more than any player he ever coached. He knew Roaf was a future Hall of Famer and was in awe of his ability.

Roaf had been the cornerstone of the offense since the Saints selected him with the No. 8 overall pick in the first round of the 1993 draft. He was a four-time All-Pro selection and a seven-time Pro Bowler.

"Willie is a future Hall of Famer," Haslett said shortly after taking over in 2000. "He's the best left tackle I've ever seen."

So when Roaf turned on him after the 2001 season, the coach felt betrayed. Indeed, team insiders say Haslett went out of his way to protect Roaf during his personal crisis.

When Roaf went A.W.O.L. during a midseason game against St. Louis, Haslett told reporters Roaf was in Colorado receiving a second opinion on his injured knee. Roaf actually was there to meet with his agent, Peter Schaffer, and to receive counseling about his troubled personal life. Within the Saints organization, coaches and executives were privately concerned Roaf had slipped into a serious bout of depression.

Roaf, meantime, lost trust in Haslett and team officials, who he felt had exacerbated the problem instead of fixing it.

The relationship between Roaf and his teammates had eroded to the point that a trade had to be made. On March 26, 2002, Roaf was unceremoniously traded to Kansas City for a conditional fourth-round draft choice.

Kyle Turley

Kyle Turley was already one of the most popular Saints, but he became a cult figure after a November 4 home game against the Jets on ESPN in 2001.

In the final two minutes with the Saints driving for the potential tying touchdown, Aaron Brooks scrambled for a short gain inside the Jets' 10-yard line. In the ensuing pile-up, Jets safety Damien Robinson latched on to Brooks's facemask and twisted it grotesquely to the side.

The six-foot-five, 300-pound Turley lost it. He dove into the pile, grappled with Robinson and ripped his helmet off. He then tossed the helmet across the field as the Superdome crowd went wild.

Officials, however, were not impressed. They assessed a pair of personal foul penalties against Turley. One of them was offset by a personal foul on Robinson. But the damage was done. Instead of a third and two at the Jets' 5, the Saints faced a second and 17 at the 20. The Saints failed to score and lost 16-9.

The loss, however, became a footnote to the helmet-throwing incident. The story went national and Turley instantly became a cult hero.

Kyle Turley became an instant cult hero after he tossed the helmet of New York Jets' Damian Robinson following a fracas in a 2001 loss at the Superdome. *Chuck Cook/The Times-Picayune.*

The Saints fined Turley $25,000 and ordered him to attend anger management classes, which, not surprisingly, angered Turley.

He grew even more surly after *The Times-Picayune* ran a feature story the following week titled "The Mad Man," chronicling his history of violent acts. The story detailed several past incidents dating back to his days at San Diego State University. It also quoted his mother, Kathy Turley, who said Turley's rage may result from a bitter divorce and the separation from his 19-month-old daughter, Haley.

"I think his divorce definitely has played a part in what you've seen on the field," Kathy Turley told the paper. "This is how he's taking it out. He thought he had every-thing—the perfect marriage, the perfect job, the perfect life—and he ended up with nothing. The divorce threw him for a loop."

Turley vowed to never speak to *Times-Picayune* reporters again. In his mind, he didn't need a good rela-tionship with the local media. And indeed he had a point. Turley was a national star now. He was a regular guest on FOX Sports' *Best Damn Sports Show Period* and Dan Patrick's ESPN radio show. *Sports Illustrated* and *ESPN Magazine* published features on him.

Turley had carefully orchestrated an image as an enforcer, a defender of the meek. The perception sold well nationally. But those that dealt with Turley on a daily basis saw another side of him that wasn't as attractive.

Turley had several run-ins with local media represen-tatives. He tried to intimidate any reporter who dared ven-ture toward his locker. After a loss to Minnesota in 2002, he purposefully and forcefully bumped a couple of reporters in the back while they were interviewing defen-sive coordinator Rick Venturi.

And Turley didn't just browbeat the media. He publicly chastised members of the media relations and community relations departments in front of their peers. His "me first" attitude gradually wore out its welcome with teammates, as well.

The Saints offered Turley a contract extension in the spring of 2003, but he blew up at general manager Mickey Loomis. A few days later, Turley blasted Loomis, owner Tom Benson and the organization on a local radio program. The club decided it had no other recourse and traded him to St. Louis for a second-round draft pick.

Aaron Brooks

On a routine Monday afternoon in early August 2000, Aaron Brooks was preparing for his second practice as the Green Bay Packers' No. 3 quarterback when Coach Mike Sherman approached him at his locker and told him he had just been traded to the Saints.

The news shocked Brooks, but there was no time to dally. He had 80 minutes to gather his clothes and valuables and catch a flight to Chicago. After a long layover and connecting flight to Charlotte, N.C., he arrived at 2:30 a.m. in Jacksonville, Florida, where the Saints were scheduled to conduct an intra-squad scrimmage against the Jaguars the following morning. Brooks underwent an hour-long physical before finally hitting the bed at 4:30 a.m.

Brooks was jolted awake by a 5:45 a.m. wake-up horn. Three hours later, wearing the practice jersey of recently cut Pat Barnes, Brooks was throwing passes with his new team.

"(The trade) totally took me off guard," Brooks said. "I showed no expression because I was so surprised. But this is a business. You've got to accept the business and how it is. I'm looking forward to the opportunity."

When the Saints first pitched the Packers about a trade for a reserve quarterback, the object of their affection was back-up Matt Hasselbeck.

Hasselbeck, a promising young passer, was off the blocks. Instead, Green Bay offered the talented but raw Brooks.

Saints general manager Randy Mueller sought advice from offensive coordinator Mike McCarthy, who'd coached Brooks the previous season in Green Bay. McCarthy didn't hesitate: "Get him."

Mueller sent linebacker K.D. Williams and a 2001 third-round draft pick to the Packers for Brooks and reserve tight end Lamont Hall.

Off the Cuff

The most controversial decision of Haslett's tenure came during the stretch run of the 2002 season.

The Saints started the season 6-1 and were the talk of the league. Even after a slight mid-season slide, they rallied to upend Tampa Bay in an emotional win on Sunday night before a national television audience.

Lost amid the postgame celebration, however, was the announcement that Aaron Brooks had suffered shoulder injury in the second quarter. He was expected to be "fine," Haslett said, but the club planned to be cautious with the injury.

And indeed Brooks seemed fine. He played well the next week in a win against Baltimore, but back-up Jake Delhomme was called on to mop up the rout.

After the Ravens win, the Saints were 9-4 and needed only one win in their final three games to earn the second playoff berth of Jim Haslett's tenure. The final three opponents—Minnesota, Cincinnati and Carolina—were mired in last place in their respective divisions, and the Vikings and Panthers games were to be played in the Superdome.

Brooks played well enough to win in a heartbreaking 32-31 loss to Minnesota and he started out OK the following week at Cincinnati. But in the second half, Brooks fell apart. He completed only two of 14 passes for 13 yards, and the lowly Bengals rallied for a win that snapped a 13-game losing streak. It was the worst loss of the Haslett era.

A week later came the nadir of the Haslett-Brooks era. Needing only a win at home against the Panthers, Brooks picked up where he left off against the Bengals. He completed only 12 of 31 passes for 145 yards with two interceptions. The Saints marched into Carolina territory eight times but managed only two John Carney field goals and lost 10-6.

Brooks was booed mercilessly during the game. The catcalls stopped only when fans lobbied for beloved backup Jake Delhomme with "We want Jake!" chants. Haslett ripped into the fans during a morose postgame press conference.

Brooks's case and Haslett's decision wasn't helped by a pair of events during the offseason. First, team officials announced that Brooks would undergo arthroscopic surgery to repair a torn tendon in the rotator cuff of his right shoulder. A couple of months later, Delhomme signed with Carolina and directed the NFC South rivals to a berth in Super Bowl XXXVIII.

The relationship between Saints fans and their head coach and quarterback has been strained ever since.

"It doesn't matter," Brooks said. "I don't care. I'm playing as well as I can. This is not Nintendo. This is not PlayStation. This is for real. ... All I can do is try to improve each time I go out on that football field. That's my concern."

Michael Lewis

There are a lot of great stories in the NFL, but few are better than the suds-to-riches story of Saints return man Michael Lewis.

Semipro. Minor leagues. Sandlot. Flag. Lewis played it all, a wide receiver for football teams like the Kenner City Chiefs, the New Orleans Thunder and the Bayou Beast.

Like an aspiring actor waiting tables, he had to pay the bills. He spent a few years pouring concrete, then took a job driving 18-wheelers. It was while driving a beer truck for a local Budweiser distributor through Baton Rouge in 1998 that Lewis heard a radio interview that perked up his ears.

Buford Jordan, the former fullback for the Saints, was the coach of a new football team in Baton Rouge, the Louisiana Bayou Beast of the Indoor Professional Football League. Jordan was looking for players. Open tryouts were that weekend.

Lewis made the team, and left his job to work as a beer distributor in Baton Rouge. He started his days at 5 a.m. and sometimes delivered more than 700 cases of beer before heading to practice.

Eventually, though, the Beast folded. Lewis worked the phones and earned a tryout with the New Jersey Red Dogs of the Arena Football League. He earned a roster spot by clocking a time of 4.19 seconds in the 40-yard dash.

Lewis parlayed that job into an invitation to spend training camp with the Philadelphia Eagles. He was released during the final round of cuts, but the hometown Saints signed him to their practice squad later that winter.

The next fall, at the age of 29, he earned a spot on his first NFL roster. When his remarkable story became public, he quickly became a fan favorite. Calls for the "Beer Man" resonated through the Superdome on every punt and kickoff return. Two years later he shattered the NFL record for combined kickoff and punt return yardage with 2,432 yards and made the Pro Bowl as well as almost every All-Pro team.

"I thought I was going to play Arena football for four or five years and come back home and start working again," Lewis said of his remarkable odyssey. "I didn't think it would go this far. My biggest goal was just to get a tryout in the NFL."

CHAPTER 8

Only in New Orleans

The Great Pizza Revolt

The food at the 1971 training camp in Hattiesburg, Mississippi, was so bad the Saints staged a walk out.

When it came time for the 7 p.m. dinner, the players checked in, paraded through the chow line, touched nothing and left the building.

"The Great Pizza Revolt," as it later became known, had begun. The players, en masse, headed to a local pizza parlor.

The entire squad, save one lone dissenter, swarmed the joint. As the squad filed in, tight end Dave Parks was heard placing his order: "Let's see, we'll have 10 anchovy, 12 mushroom, 13 pepperoni, 15 combination and one sardine. Got that?"

Fearing a fine, punter Julian Fagan stayed behind. He ate by himself at the Southern Miss cafeteria.

Coach J.D. Roberts later fined Fagan.

"I want this team to stick together," Roberts said.

Fagan's response: "I'm puzzled."

As is their wont, the Saints later tried to cover up the walk out, saying it was a pizza party to welcome Parks to camp after he had ended his contract holdout hours earlier.

The Singin' Saint

Ray Rissmiller started singing in the church choir in his hometown of Easton, Pennsylvania. He took his talent to Philadelphia-area TV shows in 1966 while playing offensive tackle for the Philadelphia Eagles. A year later, both careers took a turn when he was traded to New Orleans, where he eventually won a starting spot at left tackle and a lounge job where he was known as The Singin' Saint.

Rissmiller's act was quite a hit in the French Quarter clubs. His long blond hair flowing over his broad shoulders, Rissmiller would summon his teammates to the stage for sing-alongs to the delight of fans, who packed the joint.

Rissmiller, who described his singing style as "a mixture of Eddie Arnold and Bobby Vinton," recorded two songs, "Big Ray" and "City Lights." The recordings, he said, were "country and western with a rock beat." He debuted "City Lights" at the New Orleans Press Club in December of 1967.

"That was quite a scene," Rissmiller said. "The place was packed and people were really into it. To ride down the road and hear your song on the radio as "The Pick of the Week" was really something else. But Coach Fears didn't like it too much. I think he thought we should have spent more time lifting weights or something. But we had a ball."

Neither of Rissmiller's careers lasted very long. He was cut by the Saints in 1968. His singing career ended even sooner.

"We came back from a road trip, and the manager had made off with all of our money," Rissmiller said. "We never heard from him again."

"Number One"

Charlton Heston seemingly had done it all during his Academy Award-winning acting career. He'd competed in chariot races in *Ben Hur*. He'd parted the Red Sea as Moses in *The Ten Commandments*. And he'd painted the Sistine Chapel as Michelangelo in *The Agony and Ecstasy*.

But the great actor met his match in 1967 when he tried to play Saints quarterback Ron "Cat" Catlin in a motion picture called *Number One*.

During rehearsal sessions, Heston struggled to master even the most basic skills of quarterback play. Saints quarterback Billy Kilmer and former Southern Cal quarterback Craig Fertig worked with Heston, to no avail.

"He was the most uncoordinated man I've ever been around," Kilmer said. "I've seen women throw the ball better than him."

Trainer Warren Ariail said every spiral pass used in the picture was thrown by Saints equipment manager Charlie Shepard.

"Heston was a nice guy, but he couldn't throw a spiral to save his life," Ariail said.

Several Saints participated in the filming of the picture, including Doug Atkins, Lou Cordileone, Monty "Doctor Strangebrain" Stickles and Roy "Captain Weirdo" Schmidt. The group would shoot scenes after practice at Tulane Stadium on Monday, Tuesday and Wednesday afternoons.

Director Tom Gries wanted to make the football scenes believable, so he asked Saints defenders to rush Heston hard during their first scene.

"The guys didn't want to hurt him so they kind of just went through the motions," Kilmer said. "The director says, 'Boys, boys. We've got to do this full speed. It's got to look real.' The guys said, 'OK.'"

On the next take, an overanxious Captain Weirdo blasted Heston and broke two of his ribs.

Kilmer still has a photograph of himself and Heston sitting on tables in the training room. Kilmer is being treated for an ankle injury. Heston is receiving treatment on his ribs.

The studio shot live game action of Kilmer during the exhibition season and spliced the footage in with close-ups of Heston to make the football scenes appear realistic.

"I was the double for Charlton Heston because we were about the same height," Kilmer said. "But he was only about 160 pounds and in those days I weighed about 215. You'd see this little guy, then they'd cut away to me in a game and there'd be this huge guy running around. It was a bad picture."

Space Cowboy

In 1972, owner John Mecom hired former astronaut Richard F. Gordon Jr. as general manager. At his first news conference, Gordon stunned his listeners. "If anybody has any suggestions on how to run this football team," he said. "I'll be glad to listen.'"

Gordon had recently retired after a distinguished 20-year career in the military. A navy captain for most of his tenure, Gordon spent the final eight years as an astronaut. He commandeered the Gemini II mission in 1966 and piloted the Yankee Clipper lunar module while Alan Bean and Charles Conrad made a second lunar landing during the Apollo 12 mission in 1969.

"The image of pro football is changing, and I don't think it's necessary at all to have a man with an extensive football background," said Mecom at Gordon's introductory press conference. "In fact, I don't think any football experience is necessary to be a general manager."

Once, while negotiating a contract with wide receiver Danny Abramowicz, the Saints' best receiver, Gordon is said to have argued that he had gone to the moon for a whole lot less than Abramowicz was asking. Abramowicz responded: "That's your problem."

The Playbook Scam

People have stolen signs in baseball. And spies have pilfered football plays by sneaking into practice or using binoculars at practice. But the scam Karl Sweetan tried to implicate the Saints in was considered a crime by federal authorities.

"The Case of the Purloined Playbook," as one newspaper headline called it, unfolded in July 1972. J. D. Roberts, the New Orleans Saints coach, reported to the N.F.L. security office that Sweetan had contacted him in hopes of selling him a Los Angeles Rams playbook.

Sweetan was a back up to Billy Kilmer for the Saints in 1968. He was traded to the Rams a year later and was released in 1971. Sour grapes, perhaps, led him to solicit Roberts.

The league notified F.B.I. agents, who arrested Sweetan and a cousin while they were allegedly trying to sell the playbook to Roberts in a predawn meeting at a New Orleans motel. Sweetan and the cousin, Wayne Boswell, were handcuffed, spent a night in jail and were charged with wire fraud and interstate transportation of stolen property. The Rams, then rivals of the Saints in the NFC West division, determined that the item offered, reportedly for $2,500, was a photostat of the Rams' 1971 playbook—secrets from the previous season.

In February 1973, Gerald Gallinghouse, the United States Attorney in New Orleans, reported that the consensus of "numerous experts on pro football" he surveyed put the playbook's monetary value at less than $5,000, the threshold for the sale of a stolen object across state lines to be a federal crime. As a result, Gallinghouse did not seek indictments.

Roberts might have wanted to take Sweetan up on his offer. A few weeks later the Rams routed the Saints 34-14 in the season opener.

The Longest Boo

Roman Gabriel futilely kept putting his hands under center, but the Eagles quarterback couldn't hear his own voice, so he knew his teammates were helpless.

It was the third quarter of the seventh game of the 1974 season. But the 64,257 fans at Tulane Stadium were into it.

The Eagles had a first and goal at the Saints' 7-yard line but the crowd was incensed about a pair of personal foul calls against the home team that set up Philadelphia inside the 10-yard line.

Gabriel tried 11 times to run a play. Each time the booing escalated. Finally, officials sent both teams to the sidelines for a 10-minute breather.

The intermission didn't stop the torrent. Gabriel finally called a quick count and sneaked up the middle for a one-yard gain.

"That S.O.B. tried to fool us," defensive tackle Derland Moore said. "He was asking us to help him quiet the crowd, so I stood up to start waving and he goosed the center and tried a quick sneak."

Moore didn't take kindly to the move.

"Gabriel was cussing at us at the bottom of the pile and Derland was just wailing on him," said defensive end Steve Baumgartner. "He was punching him and clawing at his face."

The Saints defense held on the next two downs, and the Eagles were forced to settle for an 18-yard field goal by ex-Saint Tom Dempsey and a 10-7 lead.

The Saints later drove for a game-winning touchdown, a four-yard run by Jess Phillips in the final minutes, to post a 14-10 win.

The final recorded time of the delay: 22 minutes.

"We would have scored a touchdown on that series," Gabriel told reporters afterward. "The officials didn't have the guts to do what they were supposed to do."

Lost in Transportation

In their seemingly eternal search for a game-breaking receiver, the Saints acquired wide receiver Lawrence Williams during training camp of the 1975 season. The Saints traded an undisclosed draft pick to New England for Williams, a speedster who the Patriots selected in the seventh round of that spring's draft.

The Saints soon learned why a talent like Williams was expendable. Williams arrived in camp on Thursday, but failed to show for the Saints' preseason game against the Dolphins at the Superdome on Saturday.

When North confronted Williams in a meeting the next day, Williams told the coach he never was informed about the departure schedule for the team buses, then got lost en route to the stadium and couldn't find the Superdome.

"Well, I hope you can find the airport," North shot back, while giving Williams his walking papers.

North later told reporters, "I don't care what the problem was—anyone who doesn't care enough to make it to the stadium can't be serious about making this ball club. Our scouts liked him, and he was supposed to be fast, but I just can't keep a guy on the team who can't find his way to the stadium."

Class Clowns

The only thing Derland Moore liked to do more than play football was cut up and party. He and running mates Steve Baumgartner and Andy Dorris terrorized training camp during the free-wheeling mid- to late '70s.

No prank was beyond their reach. They fired tennis balls at unsuspecting teammates out of a make-shift cannon built from beer cans and starter fluid. They ambushed people with fire extinguishers and car-jacked the coaches' golf carts. Near the end of camp each fall, they would accost the team's assistant trainers, bind them in medical tape and submerge them in ice water.

"Dick Gordon, the former astronaut they hired as G.M., he liked our cannon, being an engineer and all," said Baumgartner, who roomed with Moore for most of his career. "Our room was down toward the mess hall and 90 percent of the players would have to go by our room to get to the mess hall. Our room was sort of the emporium, a big gathering spot. We'd sit in there and play cards. We'd get the cannon loaded up and crack the door open. They'd see that door open and they would see that canon come out and they knew it was coming. They'd be dead tired but they'd see that cannon and they'd start sprinting down the hall. We'd take a shot at them every day."

One of their rituals in Vero Beach was the purchase of the "camp car."

"Every year we'd go see Jimmy the Junk Man and get us a car out of the wrecking yard," Moore said. "We'd pay a couple hundred bucks for it. He'd lick an inspection sticker on it, and that's what we drove. At the end of camp, we'd just leave it there."

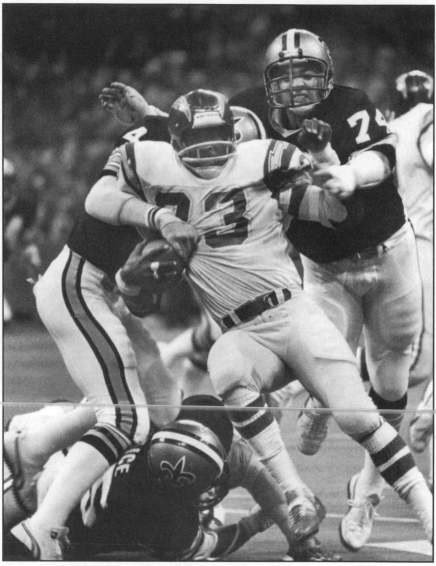

Derland Moore (74) didn't just wreak havoc on opposing teams. In the mid- to late '70s, Moore, along with teammates Steve Baumgartner and Andy Dorris, also wreaked havoc on Saints training camps with their pranks and practical jokes. *Photo courtesy of The New Orleans Saints*

One of Moore and Baumgartner's favorite "camp cars" was a 1965 Mercury Caliente Convertible. "It was so big we called it the Enterprise," Moore said. "The sun roof was a deflector shield."

One day, kicker Rich Szaro borrowed the Caliente and made the cardinal sin of forgetting to refill it with gas. Since the gas gauge was broken, Szaro had been warned to put gas in it. When it ran out on Moore's next trip and left him stranded, Szaro was doomed.

Szaro decided to strike first. The next night he ambushed Moore and Baumgartner with a fire extinguisher, then bolted to his room and locked the door.

Being the expert camp terrorists that they were, Moore and Baumgartner had procured the latest top-of-the-line chemical fire extinguishers, as well as a master key that allowed them access to every dorm room.

"I grab the smogger and the pass key," Moore said. "You could hear Szaro inside his room, yelling, 'Ha, ha. You can't get me.' We opened the door and—Whoosh! All you could see was white smoke coming out of the room. And you can hear Szaro coming out of there screaming. 'You owe me for the room.' You ruined my whole wardrobe." And he never messed with us again. There was a quarter-inch of white powder all over the room. He had to move out."

'Dilla on the Loose

The mother of all Baumgartner-Moore pranks took place in 1973 at Dodgertown in Vero Beach, Florida.

After team meetings one evening, defensive tackle Elix Price alerted Baumgartner that an armadillo was on the loose. Never one to let an opportunity pass, Baumgartner and Andy Dorris captured the mammal in a plastic garbage can.

Baumgartner, who had secretly acquired a master key to all the dorm rooms, dumped the critter in the rooms of several unsuspecting teammates for a couple of hours.

"You'd hear, 'What the hell's that?'" Baumgartner said. "Then you'd see men, professional football players, standing on beds and chairs. We entertained ourselves with this for a while."

They finally realized that one room that was left unattended—that of wide receivers Speedy Thomas and Jubilee Dunbar. Baumgartner dumped the armadillo into their room and returned to his room to go to bed.

"They come in during the course of the night and pass out," Baumgartner said. "Well, that armadillo is nocturnal and one of them saw those red eyes peering from under the bed."

Thomas bolted upright.

"Jubilee," he shouted, "There's a giant rat in the room!"

Dunbar replied, "That's no rat!" Dunbar said. "That's a 'dilla!"

The terrified players stood on their beds, firing the telephone book, a Bible and a couple of ashtrays at the equally frightened armadillo as Baumgartner and Dorris listened with great amusement.

The armadillo finally found refuge in the bathroom, where Dodgertown general manager Dick Bird found it the next day. Damage was extensive. The door had scratches and bite marks. The shower was destroyed. Towels were shreaded. Mounds of feces dotted the bathroom.

"It was disgusting," Baumgartner said.

"I hate to say that prank is the all-time greatest, because there was some hilarious stunts pulled during my time. But man, the armadillo was good," Kleinschmidt said. "It is legendary. That group of guys in the mid-'70s, late '70s, they were characters. It's tough to top some of the stories coming from that time."

Dirty Laundry

Dave Lafary was not having a good day. It was four games into his second season and he was starting at tackle in what amounted to a homecoming for Lafary in Cincinnati in 1978.

Lafary, a towering tackle who teammate Tinker Owens called "Handsome Igo," was battling the heat in the humid September air while trying to endure a severe case of diarrhea.

The Saints trailed 18-17 when they took over in the final two minutes. Just before the drive, offensive line coach Dick Stanfel huddled his troops to discuss the game plan. But Lafary was on his way to the locker room to relieve himself.

"Dave said, 'Coach, I really gotta go,'" defensive tackle Derland Moore recalls. "Dick said, 'We've got a game to win! Shit in your pants!' And he did. He did right there in a big pile up. There was a big ole brown stain in his pants. It was nasty."

Archie Manning said he can still remember Bengals linebacker Jim LeClair calling out line checks before each play during the drive.

"He'd point at Lafary and say, 'Goddamn, that's awful! You're a filthy son of a bitch!'"

Manning recognized an opportunity and ran plays behind Lafary en route to the game-winning field goal. The Saints won 20-18.

"We tried to get those pants after the game to hang them in the Hall of Fame," Moore said. "But Lafary was hosing them down as soon as we got in the locker room."

In the Bag

A legend was born during the 1-15 season of 1980. One year removed from the best record in club history, the team disintegrated. Chemistry and drug problems swamped morale and divided the roster. The Saints started the season 0-5 and were the laughingstock of the league.

Things got so bad that Bobby LeCompte couldn't stand it anymore. LeCompte, the manager/bartender at Buddy Diliberto's Buddy D's Lounge in Metairie, was catching a lot of flak from patrons because he continued to attend the dreadful Saints games.

The bag-head craze began during the grim 1-15 season of 1980 and continues to this day among the club's frustrated fan base. *Eliot Kamenitz/The Times-Picayune*

At the time, the Unknown Comic, whose schtick was to wear a brown plastic grocery bag over his head throughout his routine, was one of the top acts in entertainment.

When the Unknown Comic popped up on the screen at the bar, an idea popped into LeCompte's head. He took the idea and ran with it.

"With the Saints having a terrible year, Sunday night business was really bad," LeCompte said. "Buddy wanted an idea to kinda spruce up interest, something he could do on his show that would make things interesting, or at least funny.

"I was thinking how embarrassing it was to show your face at the stadium. At first, I thought about making a mask, then I looked at the bags laying all over the place."

Ten minutes later, ear holes, eye holes, nose and mouth holes had been cut. A helmet decal was added. LeCompte replaced the fleur de lis emblem with a question mark. For a finishing touch, LeCompte added the word "Ain'ts," because, he said, the Saints "ain't been doing nothin' all year long."

A handful of fans wore the bags to the Falcons game. The number grew to about 200 for the next home game and increased exponentially as the futility continued.

LeCompte eventually started a cottage business, selling the bags for $1 each. At the height of the craze, he was selling as many as 5,000 bags a game.

Those who didn't purchase LeCompte's bags made their own. The city's lunatic fringe embraced the idea, growing more creative and colorful with the adornment of their headware and their accompanying messages each week.

The craze reached a full-scale frenzy when the 0-11 Saints played host to the Los Angeles Rams for a Monday night game just before Thanksgiving. Creative fans turned the game into a bag-travaganza. Checkered bags. Black bags. Gold bags. Bags decorated with sequins and beads. One man came dressed in a full body bag. One couple wore a box large enough to cover both their heads.

Howard Cosell looked down on thousands of grocery bags in the stands and offered up his opinion on what a disgrace that this was to the game of football.

Diliberto, then the sports director for WVUE-TV, started wearing a bag for his Sunday night postgame show, *From The Press Box*, after the Saints started 0-5.

"Little did I imagine I'd still be wearing one seven weeks later," Diliberto said this week.

Late in the season, a fan sent him a bag with real electric Christmas lights. News director Alec Gifford suggested Diliberto open the show with the bag on his head, then producers would turn the lights on for effect.

"When they turned it on, I could hear bulbs popping and felt the shock and twinges," Diliberto said. "I thought, God, will Mecom love this—I electrocute myself on live TV!"

Howard Cosell aside, not everyone was amused by the bag display. Saints players and officials criticized the bag heads for showing a lack of class and tried to confiscate them at the Rams game by order of the fire marshal, who claimed they were not flame retardant.

"So people just sneaked them into the games in their pockets," LeCompte said. "Once inside, there were too many people wearing bags for anybody to stop them."

Double Whammy

During the John North era, players came and went at a head-spinning rate. One year the Saints had more than 120 players in training camp. The revolving door soon became a running joke amongst the veterans on the roster.

During one preseason game, the Saints had signed a return specialist who had recently been cut by the Oakland Raiders. The player arrived at the Superdome on the day of an exhibition game.

According to Saints quarterback Archie Manning, the return man arrived with a pet parrot.

"An expensive parrot, too," Manning said. "One of those birds that cost about $1,000. He came in with the parrot on his shoulder. When we went out for the game, he just stuck the parrot in his locker. We asked him if it would be OK in there by itself and he said, 'Sure, he'll be fine. He'll just sit there.'"

Unfortunately, the return man wasn't fine. On his first punt attempt, he called for a fair catch at his own 3-yard line. On his second, he fumbled.

"There wasn't a third," Manning said. "He was cut right there. Then he went in the locker room and found his parrot had died. It was a bad night all around."

Fire in Their Eyes

Based in one of the entertainment capitals of the world, the Saints know the importance of putting on a good halftime show.

They had a special celebration planned to commemorate the 25th anniversary of the franchise for a game against the 49ers on November 10, 1991.

A rocket from a fireworks exhibition struck the rafters and ignited some of the burlap used to wrap metal guidewires on the gondola below the giant screens, almost 200 feet above the field.

A blazing burlap bag plunged from the rafters onto the field late in the third quarter, resulting in an eight-minute delay.

Ray Tufts, a San Francisco assistant trainer, ran out with a small cup of water that he poured on the blaze. Two people carried a large container of ice and water from the Saints sideline and poured it on the fire. Saints official Barra Birrcher ran in from the end zone with a mat and began beating the flames.

Four New Orleans firefighters also charged onto the field to extinguish the blaze, but not before a large scorch mark was left on the AstroTurf playing surface at the 40-yard line.

Frank Sweet, a worker at Classic Fireworks, the company that produced the game's halftime fireworks show, dropped out of the Superdome roof, straddled a steel girder and single-handedly smothered the fire in the rafters 160 feet above the turf.

After the delay, Morten Andersen, who was preparing at the other end of the field, kicked a 21-yard field goal to give the Saints a 10-3 lead that proved to be the final score.

"I was looking for some weenies," Andersen said. "We had time enough for a little barbecue."

CHAPTER 9

The Infamous Decisions

Jim Taylor

John Mecom wanted to make noise in his first season as an NFL owner. In his first days on the job, he immediately targeted Green Bay Packers great Jim Taylor. The Baton Rouge native had fallen out of favor with Coach Vince Lombardi and planned to play out his option year with the Packers.

NFL rules, however, required teams that signed "option year" players to compensate the old team. A precedent was set in 1965 when Detroit was forced to award

Green Bay a No. 1 draft pick for signing tight end Ron Kramer.

Despite the compensation, Mecom didn't hesitate. Taylor was a huge star and would be a box-office bonanza in Louisiana. Sen. Russell Long and Gov. John McKeithen, both of whom were vital in luring the NFL to New Orleans, also were believed to have influenced Mecom's decision.

After an extended courtship, Mecom signed Taylor to an eye-popping four-year, $400,000 contract on July 6, 1967.

As compensation, NFL commissioner Pete Rozelle forced the Saints to give the Packers their No. 1 pick in the 1968 draft. The Packers used the pick, the No. 5 overall selection, to take linebacker Fred Carr, who went on to earn three Pro Bowl invitations.

Meanwhile, the 31-year-old Taylor played just one frustrating season before injuries forced him to retire. He led the Saints in rushing with 390 yards on 130 carries and added 38 catches for 251 yards.

"It was a shame because Jimmy was all right," quarterback Billy Kilmer said. "We just didn't have an offensive line down there. We couldn't move the ball. Jimmy sometimes would get hit four or five yards in the backfield. He never had a chance."

Fears later told *The Times-Picayune*: "That wasn't that bad a thing because I know he was a local figure and he was a great football player. But I had been with him (Taylor) at Green Bay, and I knew he was in his waning years."

Gary Cuozzo

The first major trade in Saints history set an ominous precedent.

Desperately in need of a franchise quarterback to build around, the Saints chose to trade for a proven young commodity rather than risk selecting a signal-caller with the No. 1 overall pick in the draft. Purdue's Bob Griese and Auburn's Steve Spurrier were the top draft prospects at quarterback that year. The Saints' braintrust wasn't enamored with either one of them, so the club traded the No. 1 overall pick and center Bill Curry to Baltimore for unproven but highly regarded Gary Cuozzo, the 25-year-old back-up to Johnny Unitas and guard Butch Allison.

Baltimore used the No. 1 pick to draft Bubba Smith, a future Pro Bowl defensive end from Michigan State.

Instead of drafting No. 1, the Saints had to wait until No. 26, where they took fullback Les Kelly, another major bust.

At the time, Coach Tom Fears said of the trade, "It's like trading Steve Spurrier or Bob Griese for Cuozzo."

Even if the Saints didn't select a quarterback or Smith, they could have had taken running back Floyd Little, cornerback Mel Farr, wide receiver Gene Washington, defensive lineman Alan Page, or offensive tackle Gene Upshaw.

Billy Kilmer beat out Cuozzo for the starting job in 1967. A year later Cuozzo was dealt to Minnesota for a pair of No. 1 draft picks in 1968 and 1969.

"Gary had good technique, but Billy had that emotional leadership," offensive tackle Jake Kupp said. "You had to use more of your emotional skills with our early teams. If Gary had gone to a more experienced team he might have been all right. With the type of team we had we needed that toughness that Billy brought to the team."

"I already had the quarterback I wanted (Bill Kilmer)," recalled Fears to *The Times-Picayune*. "I had wanted to build a new team of my own and we lost a No. 1 draft choice and a damned good center right off the bat."

Les Kelley

Having dealt the No. 1 overall pick in the 1967 draft to Baltimore for back-up quarterback Gary Cuozzo, the Saints desperately needed to hit a bull's-eye on their other No. 1 selection, the No. 26 overall selection.

Fears asked his scouting department for a running back or an intimidating defensive back.

When the Saints' pick rolled around, plenty of talent remained, including defensive back Lem Barney (Lions) and linebacker Willie Lanier (Chiefs). The Saints selected a husky fullback from Alabama named Les Kelley.

They picked their intimidating defensive back, Bo Burris, a safety who played quarterback in college, a couple of rounds later.

Kelley's career never got on track. He battled the measles and a knee injury during training camp and failed to carry the ball or make an official catch all season. A year later, Tom Fears announced he was moving him to linebacker.

Kelley played sparingly over the next three years before being cut in 1969. His final production count: One interception and one kickoff return for 20 yards.

"[Mecom] had already hired that scouting department," Fears told reporters years later. "They had no idea of what I was looking for. Kelley should never have been a high draft choice."

Kelley wasn't alone. Thirty of the 36 players drafted by the Saints in 1967 were out of football within three seasons.

Billy Kilmer

Most people assume Kilmer was traded because the Saints were poised to pick Ole Miss's Archie Manning with the No. 2 overall selection in the college draft.

Billy Kilmer (17) established himself as a leader and all-around tough guy in four seasons before being unceremoniously traded to Washington in 1970. *Robert T. Steiner/The Times-Picayune*

That's true, but it's not the real reason, according to longtime Saints watchdog and legendary radio personality Buddy Diliberto.

Diliberto claims there's an untold story behind Kilmer's 1971 dismissal.

It occurred the night of the Saints' ugly 24-3 loss to Chicago in the 1970 season finale. Later that evening, Kilmer ended up in a favorite French Quarter bar called The Chart Room. His date was Mecom's secretary.

"It was about midnight and everything is going fine, then all of a sudden they hear the bartender say, 'Hi, Mr. Mecom, how's things going?'" Diliberto said. "Mecom says, 'Well, Happy, if I didn't have an alcoholic for a quarterback and a blankety-blank for a secretary, it would be OK.' Kilmer heard it and swung around from behind the post and started strangling Mecom on the bar. They had to pull them apart."

The next day, according to Diliberto, Mecom ordered team officials to trade Kilmer—with one condition.

"Mecom told them, 'I never want to hear from Billy Kilmer again. I don't care what they offer—just put him someplace that you'll never have to hear from Billy Kilmer again,'" Diliberto said. "Even though San Francisco and the New York Giants were offering several more draft choices, the Saints traded him to Washington to sit behind Sonny Jurgenson."

Two years later, Kilmer led the Redskins to Super Bowl VII.

"Mecom was so bad," Diliberto said, "even when he tried to bury somebody he couldn't do it."

Larry Burton

It's difficult to screw up a Top 12 pick. It's almost impossible to whiff on two top 12 picks. Yet that's exactly what the Saints did in 1975 when Coach John North and director of player personnel Bob Whitman selected little known wide receiver Larry Burton of Purdue with the No. 7 overall pick and offensive guard Kurt Schumacher five picks later.

It was a classic case of "reaching" for a need position. The Saints were desperate for a true No. 1 receiver. They hadn't had a play-maker at the position since J.D. Roberts traded former No. 1 pick Ken Burrough to Houston in 1971.

Burton was a standout track sprinter at Purdue. But he also had a track athlete's mentality. Almost from Day One, he was hobbled by minor pulls and strains in his legs. He also owned a pair of shaky hands.

Burton played only three seasons without starting or catching more than 19 passes. He was waved in 1978.

"Larry Burton had 9.3 speed and 11.5 hands," *Times-Picayune* sports editor Peter Finney said.

Schumacher was gone after three seasons, as well.

In reaching for Burton and Schumacher, the Saints bypassed future Pro Bowlers like defensive end Gary "Big Hands" Johnson (No. 8), offensive guard Dennis Harrah (No. 11), tight end Russ Francis (No. 16), cornerback Louis Wright (No. 17), linebacker Thomas "Hollywood" Henderson (No. 18) and offensive tackle Doug France (No. 20).

Far more productive receivers Fred Soloman (round 2), Rick Upchurch (round 4) and Pat McInally (round 5) were taken after Burton.

Billy Newsome

On the day before the 1973 draft, the Saints traded the second overall pick to the Baltimore Colts for veteran defensive end Billy Newsome and a fourth-round pick, which they used to select linebacker Jim Merlo.

The Colts used the No. 2 pick to draft LSU quarterback Bert Jones. With Archie Manning entrenched at quarterback, the Saints weren't interested in Jones. But the list of serviceable players they could have selected included guard John Hannah, a future Hall of Famer, running backs Chuck Foreman, Otis Anderson and Sam Cunningham and guard Joe Delamielleure.

Newsome, a Grambling State product, was a 1970 fifth-round draft pick who started only two seasons in 1971 and 1972 and then was gone. Merlo became a serviceable player for six seasons from 1973 to 1979.

Joe Campbell

Saints officials raved about the mean streak in Maryland All-America defensive end Joe Campbell when they made him the No. 7 overall selection in the 1977 NFL Draft.

They soon discovered that Campbell's temper didn't have an off switch. His emotional flare-ups resulted in countless fights at practice and in games and numerous penalties and sideline eruptions.

He didn't adjust to the coaching staff and eventually lost his starting job to Don Reese. He was moved to training camp in 1980, then was unceremoniously traded to Oakland for a 1981 sixth-round draft pick later that year.

"He wasn't doing us much good," Saints coach Dick Nolan said. "All he was doing was getting in fights and getting kicked out of games."

Russell Erxleben

Saints coach Dick Nolan fell in love with strong-legged punter-kicker Russell Erxleben while coaching the South team at the Senior Bowl.

At Texas, Erxleben had kicked 11 field goals of more than 50 yards and three that covered over 60 yards.

Against the wishes of vice president of player personnel Harry Hulmes, the Saints made the Texas Longhorns standout the second highest drafted kicker-punter in the history of the NFL by selecting him with the No. 11 overall pick.

Two picks later, the San Diego Chargers selected future Hall of Fame tight end Kellen Winslow.

Erxleben's tenure was a disaster almost from the start. He began to complain about back and leg problems during training camp and was beaten out by Rich Szaro for the starting place-kick job.

In his first game as a Saint, his desperation pass after an errant snap from center John Watson was intercepted and returned for the game-winning touchdown in a 40-34 overtime loss to archrival Atlanta in the 1979 opener.

In the following season opener, Erxleben shanked a last-second 34-yard field goal attempt that could have tied the game in a 26-23 home loss to San Francisco.

The following morning's *Times-Picayune* featured a four-column photo of Erxleben lying face-down kicking and pounding the AstroTurf field as Joe Federspiel stared down at him dejectedly.

"By the time we got to camp the next day, somebody had taken the photo and drawn an arrow in Erxleben's back and a bow in Federspiel's hand and hung it on Erxleben's locker," Manning said. "Erxleben wasn't the most popular player on the team."

Only three other kickers have ever been selected in the first round: Charlie Gogolak (No. 6 by the Redskins in 1966), Steve Little (No. 15 by the Cardinals in 1978), and Sebastian Janikowski (No. 17 by the Raiders in 2000).

Both Erxleben and Little, who shared the NCAA record for longest field goal at 67 yards, did more punting than kicking in the NFL. Erxleben attempted only eight field goals in five years with the Saints.

Shawn Knight

As the Saints sat in the war room and the picks rattled off the TV screen in the first round of the 1987 draft, team officials couldn't believe what was taking place. Purdue cornerback Rod Woodson, a sure-fire Top 5 pick, was dropping like an anvil.

Woodson, who Saints scouts rated among the top 3 overall prospects, slid all the way to No. 10 after Philadelphia selected Jerome Brown at No. 9. With Pittsburgh eyeing a running back or linebacker at No. 10, it looked like the Saints would land Woodson.

But the Steelers knew good fortune when they saw it.

"Everybody thought Pittsburgh was going to take a running back," said former Saints director of administration Jim Miller. "When they picked Woodson the room just deflated."

The Saints quickly regrouped and turned their attention to the draft board. Three players were under consideration:

North Carolina State wide receiver Haywood Jeffires; North Carolina offensive tackle Harris Barton and Brigham Young defensive end Shawn Knight.

"Billy Kuharich was really pushing for Harris Barton," Miller said. "He said this guy is going to play in the league for 10 years. He's a solid citizen, a great player. This is the guy we ought to go with."

Finks balked. The Saints really didn't need a tackle. They already had Stan Brock at left tackle.

The defensive line, though, needed help.

"We had Bruce Clark, who was a shaky character and Tony Elliot who was a real shaky character," Miller said. "We didn't have much depth. Finks said we've got to take a defensive tackle."

So the Saints went with Knight, who Finks compared favorably to Bears standout Dan Hampton.

Knight, though, never made an impact. He reported late to camp because of contract negotiations and quickly fell out of favor.

"He never caught up," Miller said. "He didn't have very good feet, and his development was retarded from the start."

Knight failed to record a sack.

At the end of the season, Finks unloaded Knight to Denver for the Broncos 1987 first-round pick Ted Gregory, another bust.

Finks later said, "The drafting of Shawn Knight was a mistake. Now, we've got to get our coaches better players."

Steve Walsh

Jim Finks wasn't perfect. He proved that in 1987 by drafting Shawn Knight. He proved it again in 1990 when he traded three high draft picks to Dallas for back-up quarterback Steve Walsh.

Finks was forced to make the deal because the club was playing with aging veteran John Fourcade at quarterback in place of Bobby Hebert, who was mired in a season-long holdout because of a contract dispute.

Fourcade played so poorly early on that Finks panicked, dealing first- and third-round picks in 1991 and a second-rounder in 1992 for the well-regarded but unproven Walsh. The Cowboys would use those picks to build their Super Bowl championship teams.

Local reporters instantly dubbed the trade "The Lawrence Welk" deal, because, as veteran *Baton Rouge Advocate* beat reporter Sheldon Mickles said, "the Saints gave up a one and a two and a three."

Walsh never justified the deal. While he did guide the Saints to a wild-card playoff berth in the 1990 season, the Saints backed into the postseason with an 8-8 record. The Bears quickly dispatched them 16-6.

"Obviously Jim paid a heckuva lot more than he was worth," said former director of administration Jim Miller. "Walsh was still considered a good player and was very well thought of. Everybody thought that he was going to be the guy."

He wasn't. Walsh split duties with Hebert in 1991, then rode the pine for his final two seasons. He threw only 38 passes over that time and was eventually beaten out by Mike Buck for the back-up spot.

"He just never really meshed with his teammates," Miller said. "They called him Pee Wee Herman. They just never liked Walsh. He was a nice kid, a very unassuming guy, not really a take-charge guy. He never really got a lot of respect in the locker room."

Alex Molden

There was much debate in the war room when the Saints went on the clock in the 1996 NFL Draft. Even though the club had invested a second-round pick in the 1994 draft on Arizona State running back Mario Bates, there was an obvious need for help at running back. It had been six seasons since their last 1,000-yard rusher. Dalton Hilliard gained 1,262 yards in 1989. Since then, five different players had led the club in rushing.

So while the Saints clearly needed defensive help, they also knew that Heisman Trophy winner Eddie George was still on the board at No. 11.

In the end, the Saints tabbed Alex Molden, a University of Oregon standout regarded as the best cover corner in the draft. They felt Molden would team with Eric Allen and Mark McMillian in the secondary to help offset strong passing attacks in the NFC West division.

"We think Molden fits into what we've been trying to do all along on this football team—and that's improve our defense," said Bruce Lemmerman, Saints director of college scouting. "We've got a tough division to play in with San Francisco and Atlanta. Those two throw the heck out of the ball, and you've got to be able to cover to win your division. And that's what we're here to do."

The blame for drafting Molden was assigned to several scapegoats on different occasions—coach Jim Mora, defensive coordinator Jim Haslett and secondary coach Jimmy Mora. No one wanted to admit they were the one who passed over a possible future Hall of Famer to select a guy who made only eight interceptions in six seasons.

As bad as the selection proved to be, it wouldn't have been as bad as the deal the Saints tried to make that day. Before selecting Molden, team officials telephoned New England in an attempt to trade up for the No. 7 pick and select Michigan running back Tim Biakabutuka, who was drafted one spot later by NFC West rival Carolina.

"We knew Carolina, a division opponent, wanted him," said general manager Bill Kuharich. "We felt he brought a lot to the table that was special."

Kuharich declined to reveal the Saints' offer except to say it was made up of draft picks.

Jake Delhomme

Saints general manager Mickey Loomis wants to make one thing clear. The Saints wanted Jake Delhomme back on their team in the spring of 2003. But they couldn't offer the reserve quarterback the one thing he wanted: a starting job.

"Aaron Brooks was our starter, is our starter and will be our starter," Loomis said. "It was simply an issue of Jake wanting the opportunity to be a starter. It never reached the point of negotiation. It was never an issue of dollars."

Those comments hardly quelled the furor among Saints fans, who watched in frustration as their former back-up led the Carolina Panthers to Super Bowl XXXVI-II.

Delhomme's ascendance from Saints reserve to Super Bowl starter became a hot topic of debate among fans,

Quarterbacks Aaron Brooks, left, and Jake Delhomme, right, got along fine during their three seasons together in New Orleans, but the fan base quickly divided their allegiances on the pair. *Michael DeMocker/The Times-Picayune*

many of which felt Delhomme should have been given a chance to start during the team's losses to Minnesota, Cincinnati and Carolina to end the 2002 season.

Loomis said the Saints never made an official offer to Delhomme because the quarterback had made it clear he planned to test the free agent market for a chance to start with another team.

Delhomme became an unrestricted free agent on February 28, 2003. He signed a two-year, $4 million contract with Carolina on March 3 after visiting Dallas.

Delhomme's agent, Rick Smith, said the Saints discussed bringing Delhomme back for "middle-of-the-road back-up money," but that was only a last-ditch option.

"The fact that Carolina had more money and a much stronger commitment toward Jake getting a chance to start made it an easy decision," Smith said.

Delhomme said he owed it to himself and his family—his wife Keri had given birth to their first child, Lauren, a couple of months earlier in Breaux Bridge—to test free agency. He said the club's decision to not play him during the final three-game losing stretch did not affect his decision.

"I wanted a chance to compete for a job," Delhomme said. "… Certainly I was down, I was frustrated (after the 2002 season). I was more frustrated that we didn't make the playoffs. All the hard work we put in and you lose the last three games and you can't get your foot in the door."

Ironically, Delhomme credits the work of the Saints coaching staff, in particular offensive coordinator Mike McCarthy, with his development into an NFL starter.

"To be honest, he loved his relationship with Mike McCarthy and Jim Haslett," Smith said. "If you are going to point to one coach who really shaped Jake to where he is today it really is Mike McCarthy. Mike spent a lot of time with him, watching film, working on his fundamentals in the quarterback sessions. That really gave Jake a lot of confidence."

Delhomme's success in his first season as a starter has not surprised the Saints.

"We said all along that Jake was capable of being a starter," Loomis said. "None of this is surprising to us. We wish it would have been us in the Super Bowl, but we're happy for him. He's a good guy and we think his success reflects positively on the Saints."

CHAPTER 10

The Bitter Losses

Deflated Opener
September 17, 1967: Rams 27, Saints 13

An overflow crowd of 80,879 packed Tulane Stadium for the most anticipated game in New Orleans sports history.

The upstart Saints had turned the city on its head by winning five consecutive preseason games to end the exhibition season. The only team to defeat the Saints during the preseason, the Los Angeles Rams and their fabled

Fearsome Foursome defensive line, were the opponents for the home opener.

NFL Commissioner Pete Rozelle, Gov. John McKeithen, Sen. Russell B. Long, Rep. Hale Boggs and legendary jazz trumpeter Al Hirt were among the celebrities and dignitaries in attendance.

No one in the crowd that day was more proud than Dave Dixon, who watched from a seat at the 50-yard line with tennis great Dennis Ralston. The two-time NCAA singles champion from Southern Cal had just signed a contract to play in Dixon's professional tennis tour.

John Gilliam (42) played three seasons for the Saints, but never matched the excitement of his 94-yard kickoff return for a touchdown on the opening play in team history. *Photo courtesy of Bob Remy*

"It was a wonderful day," Dixon said. "I was beside myself."

The anticipation built to a crescendo during an elaborate pregame show. It reached a zenith when rookie speedster John Gilliam nestled under the opening kickoff at his 6-yard line, headed straight upfield, cut left near midfield behind a wedge of blockers and churned down the sideline in to the end zone.

Fifteen seconds into the game, and the Saints led 7-0. The crowd went into delirium. Fans spilled from the stands on to the field. And Gilliam's name was forever etched in Saints lore.

"The commissioner was on his feet cheering when Gilliam ran back the kick," Dixon said. "Even Dennis (Raltson), who was from the L.A. area and was pulling for the Rams, got excited."

Alas, the Saints failed to score another touchdown. Rams quarterback Roman Gabriel gave Los Angeles a 13-10 halftime lead on a two-yard touchdown run with one second left in the first half. The Rams, led by Gabriel's passing and their dominant defense, scored the final two touchdowns of the game to escape with the win and send home the overflow crowd disappointed.

Regardless, Gilliam's return remains one of the most exciting plays in Saints history.

"I never heard anything louder [than that crowd], before or since," said Jack Faulkner, who has the Saints defensive coordinator at the time and has worked as a scout in the NFL for more than two decades. "I don't know if a domed stadium could have handled it. I mean, you had 83,000 people all hitting high-Cs at the same time. It was a deafening, sustained sound."

Doug Atkins agreed, saying the whole scene "was a little scary."

"In my life, I've never heard that much noise at any sporting event," Atkins said. "You had about 80,000 there and all of them were about half-loaded. I thought the stands were going to fall. It was deafening."

A Date with Infamy
December 11, 1977: Bucs 33, Saints 14

The Saints weren't world-beaters in 1977, but they had reason to be confident against the hapless Tampa Bay Buccaneers.

After going 0-14 in their inaugural season of 1976, the Bucs entered the game at 0-12 and were 11-point underdogs to the 3-9 Saints. In those first dozen games, Tampa Bay had scored only 53 points and was shut out six times.

But Bucs assistant coach Tom Bass liked his team's chances when he saw Saints coach Hank Stram and owner John Mecom comparing sports coats on the field during pregame warm ups.

"Stram was saying how much his had cost and how fancy the lining was, not at all concerned about the game," Bass told *The Boston Globe*. "That's when I knew we had 'em."

For Saints quarterbacks Archie Manning and Bobby Scott, the game was a nightmare. They were sacked five times and combined to throw six interceptions, three of which were returned for second-half touchdowns.

"I was all caught up in it and throwing interceptions," Manning said. "So Hank told me at halftime, 'I want you to sit down and I'll put Scottie in. Just kind of gather your-self, and we'll put you back in there.' Well, Scottie went in there and his first pass was intercepted for a touchdown. At that point, Hank thought maybe I was gathered enough."

As the Bucs' lead mounted and the historic victory became inevitable, many among the Superdome crowd of 40,124 began cheering for the Bucs.

"It was humiliation," said Stram, who called the loss the worst of his coaching career. "Our locker room was like a morgue. It was just a bitter loss."

After the debacle, Manning and his wife, Olivia, who usually dined out after games with Patricia and Bobby Scott, improvised to deal with the hostile climate.

"I told Scottie, 'I'm not going. I'm not going out in public tonight,'" Manning said. "So we wound up going to this little steakhouse that a friend of mine owned. It had a table near the back with curtains around it. So that's where we went. And believe you me, we pulled those curtains (shut)."

Later that night, athletic trainer Dean Kleinschmidt fell asleep on his sofa in his suburban Elmwood apartment and was awakened around midnight by the *NBC Nightly News* sign off.

"The lead stories were the oil embargo in the Middle East, an auto workers strike in Detroit and the Tampa Bay Buccaneers winning their first ever game," Kleinschmidt said. "This was the world news summary. It was devastating."

On the following Monday, Stram asked the equipment manager to bring a big garbage can to the team meeting.

"The players thought I was going to give them hell about what happened," Stram said. "But I told them we're not going to look at the film. We're going to burn it up, and I threw it in the can and lit fire to it. The team just went wild. They went crazy."

The loss represented the nadir in Hank Stram's two-year tenure. He was fired a few weeks later.

Big Ben

November 12, 1978: Falcons 20, Saints 17

Finally. After a dozen years, hundreds of players, five head coaches and more than their share of heartaches, the Saints were playing a crucial late-season game with playoff implications.

The 6-4 Falcons had won four consecutive games. The 5-5 Saints were one win away from setting a franchise record for victories. The first sellout crowd since the Superdome opened in 1975 packed the stadium wearing black-and-gold "I Believe" buttons and T-shirts.

The fans were in a near state of delirium as the Saints took a 17-6 lead into the final three minutes of action. The Falcons closed to within four points on a one-yard run by Haskell Stanback with 57 seconds to play.

Still, the lead seemed safe when New Orleans recovered an onside kick at their own 49-yard line. But the Saints managed to exhaust only 30 seconds off the clock and were faced with a fourth and two at the Falcons' 43. Nolan made one of the most dubious calls in Saints history. Instead of punting and risking a block, he called for a sweep to the right by Chuck Muncie. The Falcons stuffed the play for no gain.

They took over with 11 seconds left and 57 yards of real estate between them and the goal line.

The Falcons aligned three receivers to the right of the formation and sent them all downfield. The Saints countered with seven defensive backs.

Quarterback Steve Bartkowski launched a high-arcing bomb that came down in a cluster of Saints and Falcons players at the 10-yard line, the ball popped in the air and Alfred Jackson grabbed it near the 10 and eluded three Saints defenders en route to the end zone as a stunned Superdome crowd of 70,323 gasped in disbelief.

"It was knocked right out of my hands," Saints cornerback Ralph McGill told reporters afterward. "I just about had my hands around it and it was knocked out. I was yelling, 'Leave it alone, leave it alone,' but it didn't do any good. I haven't seen anything like that since Pee Wee days."

The Falcons said they practiced the play in drills every week.

"We used to call it Big Ben," Falcons receiver Wally Francis said. "Now we call it Big Win."

The odds, Nolan estimated, were "one shot in a million."

"It's the damnedest thing I ever saw," Saints cornerback Clarence Chapman said.

States-Item beat reporter Bob Marshall called it "more than an Immaculate Reception. It was more like a Vatican Special, a Holy Rosary, a Novena and a Hail Mary rolled into one."

Defensive tackle Derland Moore remembers going to the Chart House restaurant and Pat O'Brien's with friends that night.

"I'd never seen either place so quiet on a Sunday night," Moore said. "It was like a wake. I was home by 12. Usually, we didn't get in until around 4 a.m."

The Saints finished the year at 7-9, the best mark in club history. But they also missed the playoffs for the 12th consecutive season.

"It was the biggest loss in the history of the franchise at the time because it was the most important game we'd ever played," Saints quarterback Archie Manning said. "I still can't believe it happened."

Snake Bitten
December 3, 1979: Raiders 42, Saints 35

It was Super Bowl Monday.
New Orleans was tied for first place in the NFC West Division. The Superdome was sold out. The powerful Oakland Raiders and ABC broadcasting legend Howard Cosell were coming to town.

The sting from the previous season's shocking loss to Atlanta had long since dissipated during a heady 7-6 start. This Monday night showdown against the Raiders was, quite simply, the most important game in the 13-year history of the organization.

In a franchise first, team officials were alerted by the NFL office earlier that week to begin preparations to print playoff tickets.

The Saints roared to leads of 28-7 in the second quarter and 35-14 early in the third quarter. Then the wheels fell off the jalopy.

Raiders quarterback Ken Stabler began to carve the Saints prevent defense like a pairing knife through warm Velveeta.

Oakland scored four unanswered touchdowns in the final 22 minutes to spoil the Saints' playoff hopes.

"I remember we were so fired up for that game," Saints running back Chuck Muncie said. "And we were steamrolling them, then they came back on us in the fourth quarter. I don't know what they did at halftime, but their offense was unstoppable in the second half. We (the offense) couldn't get on the field and our defense got tired. They were depleted. (Raiders wide receiver) Cliff Branch caught a couple of touchdown passes. I'll never forget, he went about 70 yards on a little hitch (pass) he caught in front of one of our defensive backs. He put a little move on and—poof!—he was gone. It was crushing."

The hangover was a doozy. Still stunned, the Saints were blasted 35-0 the following week at San Diego. To their credit, they rallied to win their season finale 29-14 against Los Angeles and preserve the first non-losing season (8-8) in club history.

"We were a high-powered offense, but we were trying to implement the flex defense," Saints quarterback Archie Manning said. "The flex was a good defense, but you have to have the right people to run it.

"We just couldn't stop people. And we just didn't know how to play with a lead. Offensively we didn't do our job. You're trying not to sit on it and at the same time trying not to give it away. It was tough."

Bum Rushed

December 18, 1983: Rams 26, Saints 24

One play. That's all the Saints needed to finish off the Rams and earn the long-overdue first playoff berth in club history.

It was fourth and three at the Los Angeles 32-yard line. Two minutes remained. With the Saints clinging to a 24-23 lead, coach Bum Phillips considered three options.

Go for the first down, which would allow the Saints to run out the clock.

Try a 49-yard field goal by Morten Andersen, who had drilled attempts from 52 and 50 yards a week earlier against Philadelphia.

Or punt the Rams deep and put the game in the hands of the league's second-ranked defense, one that hadn't allowed a first down since the first quarter.

In one of the most controversial decisions in club history, Phillips opted to punt.

Saints fans will never forget the chain of events that unfolded next.

First, back-up punter Guido Merkens, subbing for injured starter Russell Erxleben, tried a coffin-corner boot but sent the ball into the end zone. The Rams started their drive at the 20 with 1:51 to play.

Vince Ferragamo, operating against a soft prevent defense, completed four consecutive passes, then two more after two incompletions and a 15-yard personal-foul penalty to bring his team to a second down at the New Orleans 25 with six seconds left.

From there, Mike Lansford, who had been on the injured list through the first 12 weeks of the season, kicked his fourth field goal of the season.

The defeat devastated the Saints. A victory would have meant their first winning season in 17 years and their first chance to participate in the playoffs.

"We were right in our own backyard, when we were supposed to be at our toughest," defensive tackle Derland Moore said. "It still haunts me to this day. That one hurt the worst."

The Rams offense had failed to score a point until Lansford's field goal. Los Angeles's other scores came on two interception returns for touchdowns, a punt return for another score and a safety.

"There was no reason to think the Rams could go 80 yards in their last drive," Phillips said, defending the defining moment of his Saints career. "That's why we made the decision to try to punt the ball out of bounds; instead, it went into the end zone."

And once again, Saints fan went into a state of disbelief and depression.

"I'm not that good at remembering games, but that one I remember," Saints athletic trainer Dean Kleinschmidt said. "There are guys that will tell you even though he continued to coach until December of 1985 Bum Phillips quit coaching after that game. It was that devastating."

Coulda, Woulda, Shoulda
October 25, 1987: 49ers 24, Saints 22

For Saints fans, it was just another heartbreaking loss to the 49ers. Been there, done that.

For coach Jim Mora, it was the breaking point.

The Saints had dominated the 49ers for most of the afternoon but were forced to settle for five Morten Andersen field goals. Andersen missed on his team record-tying seventh attempt, a 52-yarder with two seconds left that would have lifted the Saints to victory and into a tie for first in the NFC West division.

Instead, the Saints fell for the 11th time in their last 14 games against the rival 49ers.

The loss dropped the Saints' record to 3-3 and touched off a volcanic eruption from Mora in his postgame press conference.

"The Saints ain't good enough," he said. "It's that simple."

Mora took it to another level when a reporter told him 49ers coach Bill Walsh said the Saints "looked like a playoff team."

"How can you even say something like that?" Mora asked incredulously. "The New Orleans Saints haven't had a winning season in 21 years. How can you even think about that?

"This has been the worst franchise in the history of the National Football League. For 21 years. That's ridiculous."

When asked how he felt, Mora erupted.

"I'm pissed off right now," he said. "You bet your ass I am. I'm sick of coulda, woulda, shoulda, coming close, if only."

Saints quarterback Bobby Hebert remembers the sting from the loss like it was yesterday. He also remembers the ringing in his ears of Mora's emotional, invective-laden postgame harangue.

"That's exactly what we needed," Hebert said. "Nothing against (previous Saints coach) Bum (Phillips), but he was kind of light-hearted. If we would have lost that game when he was coaching he would said, 'You know what, it was a close game. We played hard. We'll get 'em next time.'

"If players could respond to that it would be great. But with the character of our team, you had to be a jerk to them. The team needed a Mora personality. He gave us that speech and we won nine straight games."

Playoff Putdown
January 3, 1988: Vikings 44, Saints 10

The fever and anticipation that swept the city of New Orleans the week of their first ever playoff game was unprecedented.

Lines began forming Sunday afternoon after the team's regular-season win against Green Bay at the Superdome for the 23,000 playoffs tickets that went on sale Monday morning. The tickets sold out in two hours.

Pious fans noted the Saints had not lost since Pope John Paul II made an appearance at the Superdome in

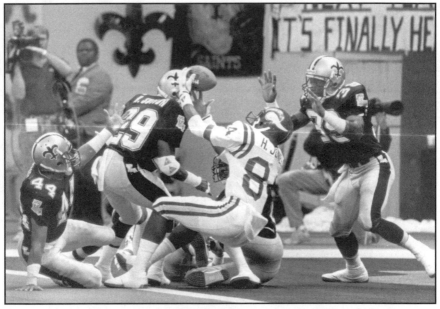

Hassan Jones caught this Hail Mary pass for a touchdown on the last play of the first half to give Minnesota a shocking 31-10 halftime lead against the Saints in the 1988 NFC playoff game. *Eliot Kamenitz/The Times-Picayune*

September. Coincidentally or not, after the visit, the Saints reeled off a club-record nine consecutive wins.

"He blessed the Saints and we've been winning since," said veteran jazz man and longtime Saints fan Pete Fountain. "This is unbelievable. You keep pinching yourself to see if this is true. We went from the outhouse to the penthouse."

The heady stay didn't last long.

The Vikings backed into the playoffs at 8-7, having lost three of their final four games. But they had dominated the Saints 33-17 the previous season and during the first half of an exhibition win earlier that year.

Lost amid the pregame euphoria was a silent warning from *Times-Picayune* columnist Dave LaGarde: "Drawing a logical conclusion from the [two losses], I'd say the Saints do not match up very well with Minnesota."

LaGarde's prediction proved prescient.

The Saints sent the sellout crowd into a frenzy by scoring a touchdown on their first series. Then it all unraveled.

Mel Gray fumbled a punt deep in his own territory to set up an early Minnesota field goal, then Anthony Carter returned a punt 84 yards for a score, and the Vikings had a 10-7 lead they would never relinquish.

Minnesota added two more scores to make it 24-10 inside the final minute of the first half. The half apparently ended on a meaningless short run by Darrin Nelson to the Saints' 49. But New Orleans had 12 men on the field, giving Minnesota time for one more play from the Saints' 44.

Wade Wilson lofted a Hail Mary that Hassan Jones pulled out of the mad scramble while falling into the end zone for a shocking 31-10 halftime lead.

The stunned Saints failed to score in the second half.

The final numbers were staggering: The Vikings out-
gained the Saints 417 yards to 149 and 28 first downs to
nine while forcing six turnovers, including four interceptions.

"That was the only playoff game that I thought the
other team was better than us," quarterback Bobby Hebert
said. "Looking back and watching the film, their defense
was just awesome."

Today, Mora blames himself for the loss.

"We were a tired team going into that game," Mora
said. "We weren't as good as we should have been, and it's
my fault. We had worked hard all year. I should have eased
up on them the last few weeks of the season. But I pushed
them too hard and we went in tired."

Bearish Afternoon
January 6, 1991: Bears 16, Saints 6

The Saints' second playoff game in franchise history
was about as ugly as a postseason game gets.

The two teams combined for nine penalties, four
turnovers and just one touchdown.

The only thing more appalling was the cold, gray
Chicago weather.

Each team played without its regular starting quarterback.

Mike Tomczak started for the Bears in place of injured
regular Jim Harbaugh and managed to avoid any costly
mistakes. That didn't keep the fans from lampooning him
with a banner that read: "Tomczak, if you were a Saint, we
wouldn't be sinners."

The Saints duo of Steve Walsh and aging veteran John
Fourcade was abysmal. Walsh completed six of 16 passes

for 74 yards and one interception. Fourcade was worse. Replacing the injured Walsh in the second half, he completed five of 18 passes for 79 yards and two interceptions.

Still, the Saints hung around and managed to pull within 10-3 on a field goal by Morten Andersen in the third quarter.

The visitors appeared to tie the game on a 61-yard return of a blocked field goal by Vince Buck, but the score was nullified by an offsides infraction against the Saints' Robert Massey.

The Bears took advantage of the mistake and tacked on another field goal for a 13-3 lead. It was all the points Chicago would need against the hapless Saints offense.

The loss extended the number of games in which the Saints failed to score more than 17 points in a game that season to ten. In 12 games, they failed to score a touchdown in the second half.

The main problem was at quarterback. Regular starter Bobby Hebert sat out the entire year because of a contract dispute with general manager Jim Finks.

As a result, the Saints finished the season ranked 23rd in total offense and 26th in passing offense. The rankings were the lowest for the club in five seasons and well below the respective marks of 11th and 13th the previous year with Hebert in command.

"There's no question we would've been better had Bobby Hebert played," Saints coach Jim Mora said. "We went three games with John Fourcade and we couldn't even get it in the end zone. We had a hard time making a first down. And we had a terrific team, but John didn't play well.

"Then we made the big trade for Steve Walsh. We probably gave up more than we should have, but we had to have a quarterback. So then it takes him a while to learn

the offense and he's really playing for the first time in the
NFL, because he didn't play much at Dallas. It was a tough
year. We had a good football team but we had some problems at quarterback. Had Bobby been there as our guy it
would have made a big difference."

Gunned Down
December 28, 1991: Falcons 27, Saints 20

Saints fans hoped to win the team's previous playoff
appearances against Minnesota and Chicago. But they
expected to win this one.

The Saints rolled into the playoffs on the crest of their
first division title and behind the NFL's second-ranked
defense. They had won five of their final seven games.
More important, starting quarterback and fan favorite
Bobby Hebert was back under center after missing time
with a shoulder injury.

The Saints led for most of the game before Atlanta
tied the score at 20 on a Norm Johnson field goal with
7:43 to play.

The score remained tied inside the final three minutes
when New Orleans' aggressive defense went for the knock-
out blow. The Saints sent safeties Vencie Glenn and Bennie
Thompson on a blitz. But quarterback Chris Miller beat it,
finding speedster Michael Haynes in single coverage
against Milton Mack. Haynes caught the ball at the
Falcons' 45, then spun toward the middle of the field
where he sidestepped Mack and eluded linebacker Sam
Mills en route to a 61-yard scoring reception.

When Haynes approached the line of scrimmage he
noticed that cornerback Milton Mack was playing far off
of him. That meant he was supposed to run a seven-yard

A dejected Bobby Hebert leaves the Superdome field after yet another first-round playoff defeat, this time a bitter 27-20 loss to Atlanta in 1991. *G. Andrew Boyd/The Times-Picayune*

hitch pattern, running downfield then quickly coming back to the ball. He did, and after making the catch at the 45, he juked Mack and ran past him and away from everyone else.

"I just got around him and outran everybody," said Haynes, a New Orleans native.

Miller completed 18 of 30 passes for 291 yards against a makeshift Saints secondary that played without starting cornerbacks Toi Cook and Vince Buck, who were injured the previous week. Mack and the much traveled Mark Lee, playing for his third team of the season, started in their place—not the best situation against Atlanta's high-powered Red Gun attack.

"I know we were better than them," Hebert said. "In the regular season we killed them (27-6 in Atlanta). You have to have depth. The difference between our starters and our backups was like night and day. Lee and Mack, they were getting burned the whole game. You put those cornerbacks out on an island. They got exposed and got burned."

The Saints' painful playoff slide continued: Three playoff appearances without a victory.

"We just (expletive) up," Saints wide receiver Eric Martin said moments after the shocking loss. "We had opportunities. We just (expletive) up."

Jim Mora later called the loss his toughest as a coach.

"This is not an excuse, but it's partly the reason," Mora said. "We had a lot of injuries in the secondary and Atlanta ran that run and shoot (offense) with those four wide receivers. I know we brought in a couple of guys the week before the playoffs or the week of the playoff game and they had to play. I hated losing to Atlanta anyway, then to have to play against the run and shoot with a banged-up secondary. That was tough."

The Futility Continues
January 3, 1993: Eagles 36, Saints 20

The lead was a commanding 20-7 with 5:15 remaining in the third quarter in the NFC Wild-Card Playoff Game. The Saints seemed headed toward their first post-season victory.

A portion of the sellout crowd of 68,000-plus broke into their familiar taunt: "Who Dat say gonna beat dem Saints? Who Dat? Who Dat? ..."

The Philadelphia Eagles answered the question with a vengeance, scoring 29 consecutive points in the final 16 minutes to stun New Orleans and deliver the most painful blow yet in the club's bitter series of playoff setbacks.

The comeback was fueled by Saints mistakes. Quarterback Bobby Hebert threw three interceptions, one of which was returned by Eric Allen for a touchdown late in the fourth quarter for the final margin. He was also sacked for a safety by Reggie White earlier in the Eagles' 26-point fourth-quarter fury.

"Is this the Louisiana voodoo curse?" Saints corner-back Vince Buck asked reporters afterward. "Because it's not this team or it's not this staff. I don't know what it is."

In the first half, the Saints accounted for 250 yards total offense. In the second half, they were held to 38 yards before padding the final statistics with a 72-yard drive to the Philadelphia 8 in the waning seconds.

Hebert sparkled in the first half, completing 13 of 19 passes for 187 yards and a seven-yard touchdown to Quinn Early. In the second half, he completed 10 of 20 passes for 104 yards, but many of those yards came after the issue had been decided.

"I had an awesome first half, but we didn't make the adjustments at halftime," Hebert said. "Their pass rush was getting to me, and we couldn't get a freaking thing done on offense. We couldn't run it on them and that allowed them to come after me."

Philadelphia, meantime, appeared to wear down the aging Saints defense, amassing 228 yards in the last two quarters.

"That was probably the most disappointing loss of my career," Hebert said. "My wife, she went and hid in the janitor's closet at the Superdome until I was done so people wouldn't bug her."

The defeat meant another squandered opportunity for the team's collection of venerable veterans, including nose tackle Jim Wilks, outside linebacker Rickey Jackson, tackle Stan Brock, tight end Hoby Brenner, defensive end Frank Warren, tight end John Tice and linebacker Sam Mills, among others.

"The Eagles game was the worst game of my life," said former director of administration Jim Miller. "I knew that was the end of our run right there."

Pointless

December 21, 2003: Jaguars 20, Saints 19

One person didn't witness the wild, last-second 75-yard touchdown that miraculously brought the Saints within an extra point of overtime and perhaps the most unbelievable comeback in club history.

John Carney didn't see Donte Stallworth start the four-player, three-lateral parade to the end zone. And he didn't see Jerome Pathon dive into the end zone to complete the score that will be replayed forever in NFL lore.

Lost between the pandemonium on the Saints' sideline and the disbelief in the partisan Jaguars crowd of 49,207 at ALLTEL Stadium, the Saints' kicker quietly and methodically went about his duty, head down, intently kicking a ball into a practice net.

Seconds later, Carney's diligence turned to disaster. He pushed the routine extra-point attempt wide right, turning what could have been a magical come-from-behind win into a stunning 20-19 defeat that eliminated the Saints (7-8) from playoff contention.

"Utter shock, that's a good way to put it," Carney said. "I can't believe it myself. As far as kickers are concerned, that's as bad as it gets."

The miss was Carney's first miss of an extra-point attempt in more than four years. It was the first time he'd missed an extra-point attempt without it being blocked in more than a decade. His only two misses since 1993 resulted from blocks—one in 1995 and another in 1999, both as a member of the San Diego Chargers.

"Everything was fine," Carney said. "I just came out of the kick early and pushed it. There's no excuse for it."

Before the miss, Carney had made 403 of 408 extra-point attempts in his 14-year career, a success rate of 98.8 percent.

"I have never, ever been a part of something like that," tight end Walter Rasby said in a stunned and sober Saints locker room. "Nothing in the NFL is a foregone conclusion, but c'mon, that's a foregone conclusion."

Incredibly, Carney's miss wasn't even the most improbable play of the day.

Trailing 20-13 at their own 25, the Saints were down to their last gasp. Six seconds remained when Aaron Brooks lined up in the shotgun for a play called "All Go Special," featuring Deuce McAllister, Michael Lewis and

John Carney had made 403 of 408 extra-point kicks in his 15-year career before inexplicably pushing one wide right in a stunning 20-19 loss to Jacksonville in 2003. *Scott Threlkeld/The Times-Picayune*

Pathon aligned to the left and Donte Stallworth alone on the right side.

Stallworth hauled in the Brooks pass near midfield, broke a pair of tackles, then reversed field to the left where he lateraled to Lewis at the 33. Lewis ran toward the Saints' sideline, but was cut off by pursuit at the 26, where he pitched the ball to McAllister. He ran five yards before being swarmed by defenders. As he was being tackled, McAllister tossed a spiral to his right that hit Pathon in stride at the 21. Pathon got a key block from Brooks on Hugh Douglas and raced untouched into the end zone as the crowd stood transfixed in disbelief.

Officials reviewed the play, but ruled that all three laterals were legal.

"It was very wild," Jaguars coach Jack Del Rio said. "The only thing missing was the band. It was kind of like the Cal game (vs. Stanford in 1982)."

The River City Relay, as it become known, was later honored as the NFL Play of the Year at Super Bowl XXXVIII.

"All the plays were great," said former Bears and Saints coach Mike Ditka, who presented the award. "But this was a phenomenal play. In the history of the NFL, you may not see anything like it again."

Added McAllister, who accepted the award in Houston on behalf of the Saints organization, "It was truly an amazing play. If we win that game, then that play definitely has to rank up there high with any other play in the history of the game."

CHAPTER 11

The Great Wins

Breaking the Ice: The First Win
November 5, 1967: Saints 31, Eagles 24

The enthusiasm of the Saints' debut season had long since died by the time the Eagles came to town in Week 8.

The high expectations raised during a 5-1 preseason were quickly doused by an 0-7 start to the regular season. The skid included three excruciating losses by a touchdown or less.

The previous week the Saints carried a 10-0 lead into the fourth quarter against Pittsburgh only to see it vanish in the final 15 minutes.

A season-low crowd of 59,596 turned out at Tulane Stadium to witness the Walter "Flea" Roberts Show.

The diminutive speedster returned the opening kick-off 91 yards for a touchdown and added two more scores on the afternoon. He scooped up a Jim Taylor fumble and raced 28 yards for a touchdown in the second quarter. Then, after the Eagles had closed the margin to 24-17 in the fourth quarter, he caught a 49-yard bomb from Gary Cuozzo to seal the first win in franchise history.

Roberts's touchdown marked the first Saints score in the fourth quarter that season.

"We figured we'd simply have to outscore the Eagles to win, and we did just that," Fears told reporters afterward after being presented the game ball by team captain Steve Stonebreaker.

For Roberts, the performance was noteworthy, considering he didn't even play the previous week against Pittsburgh while serving National Guard duty at Grambling State University.

"Man, you never really know in this game," Roberts said. "Last week at this time I was with the National Guard. I watched one quarter at the stadium and heard the rest on the radio. It was really frustrating."

Tackle Ray Rissmiller, a Pennsylvania native who played for the Eagles in 1966, was particularly happy about the win.

"We had played so many close games we knew that somewhere, somehow we were due to get that first win," Rissmiller said. "To get that first win against the Eagles was doubly sweet for me because they had traded me the previous year."

Kilmer's Pick Six
November 2, 1969: Saints 51, Cardinals 42

I t was the perfect day for an ambush.

The Saints limped into Busch Stadium with an 0-6 record. Moreover, their anemic offense had failed to score more than two touchdowns in a game all season.

Speculation about Coach Tom Fears's job security began to run rampant.

"I got it from (player personnel director) George Owen that they were going to fire Fears," Kilmer said. "I was pissed off. I was ready to play that game. The Cardinals didn't have a great defense so I knew we could move the ball on them."

Did they ever.

Kilmer threw a career-high six touchdown passes during a 345-yard passing day. He threw two scoring strikes each to Danny Abramowicz (five and 11 yards), Dave Parks (25, 13) and Ernie Wheelwright (20, one).

"I actually threw seven touchdown passes, but one was called back because of a penalty," Kilmer said. "They said I stepped over the line (of scrimmage) on a scramble to my right."

During the second and third quarters, the Saints scored 30 consecutive points to erase a 14-7 deficit.

Cardinals quarterback Charley Johnson matched Kilmer with six touchdown passes of his own while desperately trying to play catch-up.

The 12 combined touchdown passes by Kilmer and Johnson broke the previous NFL record of 11 set by the Giants and Redskins in 1962. The mark remains an NFL record.

"Charley kept coming back at us," Kilmer said. "Our cornerbacks were really struggling to stop their receivers, and finally our free safety, Dave Whitesell, told (defensive coordinator) Jack Faulkner, 'Let me play cornerback, I'll stop 'em.' They put Whitesell over there and they ran right by him, too."

The 51-point outburst was uncharacteristic of the offensively challenged Saints. In their previous 34 games they managed to score more than 30 points three times and had never scored more than 31.

Cardinals coach Charley Winner called the game "my most embarrassing moment as a coach."

The Kick Heard
Round the World
November 8, 1970: Saints 19, Lions 17

Tom Dempsey didn't even look up.

Special teams coach Don Heinrich called for a field goal and it was Dempsey's job to give it his best shot. He didn't even try to count the distance from the goal posts, which appeared notably tiny in the distance that November afternoon.

Dempsey knew he was far away. He just didn't know how far.

The Saints needed a miracle. The Lions, who trailed for most of the afternoon, had taken a 17-16 lead on an Errol Mann 18-yard field goal with 11 seconds left.

Saints receiver Al Dodd returned the ensuing kickoff to the 28-yard line, leaving six seconds on the clock, time for one play. Bill Kilmer fired a quick 17-yard strike to Dodd to take the ball to the 45. Two seconds remained. The Saints were out of timeouts.

"J.D. Roberts was yelling for an alley-oop pass but we were still too far away," Kilmer said. "Then Don Heinrich said go get the field goal team, he can kick it. It was calm with a gentle breeze that day. I remember Detroit players were laughing at us."

Holder Joe Scarpati purposefully marked the ball eight yards behind the line of scrimmage at the 37, a yard farther back than normal. He asked the line to hold their blocks a second longer than usual to give Dempsey time to wind up.

Many in the crowd of 66,910 at Tulane Stadium that day had already made their way to the exits. The ones who remained in the half-empty stadium stared in disbelief as Dempsey measured off his steps for the seemingly fruitless 63-yard attempt.

"I always believed I'd make the kick when I went out," Dempsey said. "I thought, 'just hit it sweet,' and as soon as it left my foot I knew I'd hit it well."

Players on the field that day say they still can hear the percussion of Dempsey's kick. The ball sailed high and true, eventually carrying a yard past the cross bar as the slack-jawed Lions players stared in disbelief.

"When he kicked it I said, 'Damn, he made this thing,'" Kilmer said. "I had seen Dempsey kick a 70-yarder in practice in Denver, so I didn't question the decision at all."

Dempsey's historic kick gave the Saints a miraculous 19-17 win and obliterated the previous NFL record field goal of 57 yards by Baltimore's Bert Rechichar more than a decade earlier.

"Unbelievable," Lions kicker Errol Mann said. "He could stand there and kick it 200 times and not hit (it) that sweet again. There was a wind up high in the stadium that helped him out, but I still didn't think he would make it."

The kick boosted the morale of the Saints, who were 1-5-1 entering the game. Alas, it was only temporary. The Saints lost their final six games by an average margin of 17 points.

"When he made it, everybody ran for Dempsey, and I ran straight for the locker room," Kilmer said. "I got shaved and showered and was gone while everybody was still out on the field. When I left the stadium, people were still in the stands celebrating and Dempsey was still running around the field. I was in the Absynthe House 30 minutes after the game. When I walked in, the bartender asked me, 'Did you play today?'"

Superman Wears No. 8
September 19, 1971: Saints 24, Rams 20

As debuts go, they don't get much tougher than Archie Manning's NFL indoctrination.

The former Ole Miss star was hailed as the franchise savior after being selected with the No. 2 overall pick in that spring's draft. The expectations were enormous. Saints fans had placed the hopes of their forlorn franchise on his spindly shoulders.

The Saints' opening-day opponent was the L.A. Rams, one of the favorites to win the NFL championship. The Saints had lost all four of their previous games against the Rams by at least 13 points. The Rams featured the game's most dominant defensive line, The Fearsome Foursome, that included All-Pros Deacon Jones and Merlin Olson.

If that wasn't enough, Manning had missed vital practice time during the preseason because of a foot injury he suffered while slamming into a concrete sideline dugout at Tulane Stadium.

Gulp!

Los Angeles entered the game as a 12-point favorite, but the Saints hung tough on an oppressively hot afternoon. They trailed 20-17 when Manning took over at his own 30-yard line with 1:24 to play. The rookie calmly and methodically marched the home team to the Rams' 1-yard line, where Manning called timeout with three seconds left.

"I got over to the sideline huddle with J.D. (Roberts) and Ken Shipp, our offensive coordinator, and the first thing J.D. says is, 'Let's go for it,'" Manning said. "We got that squared away. We couldn't decide which formation we were going to use, and we were kicking around different plays. Then all of a sudden the official comes over and says, 'Let's go, let's go.' Well, Danny (Abramowicz) walks out on the field with me and says, 'What are we going to run?' I said, 'They never told me.' So I kind of reverted back to my college days and called a run-pass option and just kind of bootlegged it around the end."

Manning was hit just as he crossed the goal line and lost the ball in the end zone, but officials ruled that he had crossed the plane before fumbling. Touchdown. Saints win 20-18.

The Manning legacy was born.

"I might have made a mistake because I really never thought about the pass part," Manning said. "I thought, just one yard, if I can get a good block I'm just going to get it in there. So, I went over and just dove. I knew I was over, but the crowd just didn't respond much and the officials didn't call it right away. Thank God they thought I was over."

In the next day's *Times-Picayune*, sports editor Bob Roesler wrote, "Yes, America, there is a Superman. His name is Archie Manning and he wears a Saints uniform."

Birth of the Dome Patrol
November 9, 1986: Saints 6, Rams 0

If there were any doubts that something special was happening with the Saints defense in 1986, they were removed after a 6-0 demolition of the NFC West-leading Los Angeles Rams at the Superdome on this Sunday.

The Saints didn't just beat the Rams—they strangled them. They beat them at their own game, on the ground and in the trenches.

The Saints held All-Pro running back Eric Dickerson, the league's rushing leader, to a season-low 57 yards on 21 carries. They forced five turnovers, including an interception at their 8-yard line by cornerback Dave Waymer in the closing minutes, and had three sacks.

It was the Saints' first shutout in four years. It also marked the first time the club had scored in single digits and still won. Before Sunday, the Saints had scored nine points or fewer in 54 games and lost every time.

"When we get 14 points, we can win the ball game," linebacker Rickey Jackson said afterward. "We're definitely getting to be that kind of defense."

The Rams entered the game with the league's second-ranked rushing offense. Dickerson was on pace to surpass his record-setting 2,105-yard season in 1984. His 1,141 yards entering the game was more than the entire Saints team.

But the Saints were starting to grow more comfortable and confident in coordinator Steve Sidwell's 3-4 defensive scheme. USFL imports Sam Mills and Vaughan Johnson and rookie linebacker Pat Swilling were emerging as playmakers and leaders.

Hits like this by defensive end James "Jumpy" Geathers helped the Saints limit All-Pro running back Eric Dickerson to a season-low 57 yards on 21 carries in a 6-0 shutout in 1986. *Alexander Barkoff/The Times-Picayune*

Over the last five weeks, the Saints had climbed from 23rd against the run to a solid fourth, from an average rushing yield of 137.6 yards after their first five games to only 63 in the last five.

"We shut Dickerson down totally," linebacker Vaughan Johnson said. "He didn't seem to be having all that much fun."

In the scoreless first half, Dickerson lost a fumble at the Saints' 16 and was dumped for a six-yard loss by Waymer from the Saints' 5. In the second half, he gained only eight yards. He was averaging 127 a game.

Afterward, Dickerson told reporters that he was "too tired" to talk.

Rams quarterback Steve Dils said the Saints "hit me as hard as I've been hit in a long time."

The catalyst was the smallest player on the field: five-foot-nine middle linebacker Sam Mills, who was starting to make a name for himself after signing with the Saints in August. Mills made a game-high 10 tackles.

The Rams had only been shut out twice in the previous four and a half years: 24-0 by eventual Super Bowl champion Chicago in 1985 and 37-0 by eventual Super Bowl champion San Francisco in 1984.

"There was a period there where people could not run the ball on our defense," Saints coach Jim Mora said. "We'd go into a game and a team would try to establish the run, and we'd stuff it."

After the scintillating performance, Jackson shoved a ball into the gut of defensive coordinator Steve Sidwell, saying, "That's your game ball, Coach."

Winners at Last
November 29, 1987: Saints 20, Steelers 16

Rickey Jackson knew what was coming as soon as he saw Robert Pollard enter the Steelers huddle.

The Saints were clinging to a 20-16 lead late in the fourth quarter. The Steelers were one yard away from taking the lead with a go-ahead touchdown.

"Once I saw Pollard on the field, I knew the play they were going to run," Jackson said.

The play was called "19-X," a pitch to Pollard around left end. The reserve running back never reached the line of scrimmage. Linebackers Sam Mills and Vaughan Johnson and a pack of Saints gang-tackled him one yard short of the end zone.

"We were hollering out the play before he even got the ball, then we stuffed him at the line," Jackson said.

The Steelers threatened again in the final minute, but Dave Waymer picked off a short slant pass intended for Calvin Sweeney at the Saints' 4-yard line as time expired.

The win raised the Saints' record to 8-3 with four games to play, ending a streak of 20 consecutive non-winning seasons. (A 24-day players strike canceled one game of the 16-game season.)

"We made history today," Saints owner Tom Benson said.

After the game, Dave Waymer, whose last-second interception had sealed the win, cried at his locker. Waymer, along with Stan Brock, was one of just two player left from the grim 1-15 season of 1980.

Peter Finney wrote so eloquently in The *Times-Picayune* the next day, "The story Sunday was not that the

Saints went into enemy territory and beat a Super Bowl contender. The story was that they beat a mirror image of themselves by playing 'Steeler football'—with chest-to-chest defense, by forcing six turnovers, ultimately with the kind of game-saving defensive plays that you know brightened the heart of a football primitive such as Jim Mora."

Mora gave an impassioned speech to the team in the postgame locker room.

"That's the happiest I've ever seen Coach Mora," quarterback Bobby Hebert said. "I remember he was crying like Dick Vermeil. You couldn't help but get choked up. He said, 'This meant a lot. Nobody can ever tell you again that the Saints don't have a winning season!' It was awesome."

The following week, the Saints crushed Tampa Bay 44-34 at the Superdome to clinch a wild-card spot in the playoffs for the first time ever.

"I walked into that locker room and saw guys like Stan Brock and Rickey Jackson and Dave Waymer—guys that had been there during the down years—get emotional," Mora said. "I loved watching their faces. They were now winners."

"I still have the game ball from those games," quarterback Boby Hebert said. "They're some of my favorite momentos."

Champions at Last
December 22, 1991: Saints 27, Cardinals 3

Jim Mora stood on a bench in the emotional postgame locker room and delivered an impassioned speech to his team in the wake of their rout against the Cardinals at Sun Devil Stadium.

"No one can ever take this away from you!" Mora shouted, holding the game ball above his head.

It took a quarter of a century to do it, but the Saints finally won a pennant.

To win, the Saints needed help from Dallas and got it when the Cowboys beat the Falcons 31-27 in a game that ended just after the kickoff here. Had Atlanta won, it would have finished 11-5—the same as New Orleans—but would have won the crown because the Falcons owned a better intra-division record.

"Obviously it was a great win for our team and our organization," Saints coach Jim Mora said. "I'll admit it. My eyes are wet. It's an emotional game and it gives you a great feeling to accomplish what we accomplished today."

Saints quarterback Bobby Hebert said Mora "was as emotional as I've ever seen him."

"I think it meant a lot to him since we'd always had to play second fiddle in the division to the 49ers," he added.

The Saints benefited from seven Phoenix turnovers, including five interceptions. Three of the picks were made by safety Gene Atkins, tying a club record set by Tommy Myers (1978) and Dave Waymer (1985).

"When someone told us that Dallas had won the game, it seemed like everything went up," Atkins said. "The defense and offense got fired up. That's when the guys started getting psyched and getting hurries on the quarterback. The interceptions started coming and everything started rolling our way."

When the Saints returned to New Orleans on Sunday, they were greeted by a line of fans that numbered in the thousands stretched for more than two miles at the New Orleans Airport. People carrying signs, umbrellas and replicas of Saints helmets danced and sang as they waited for the plane's arrival.

"We are right on track," linebacker Sam Mills said. "I think the city of New Orleans ought to celebrate. They deserve it. It's hard to win a championship."

Cinderella Story
November 26, 2000: Saints 31, Rams 24

Jim Haslett set the tone against the defending Super Bowl champions on the opening kickoff.

The brash head coach called for an onside kick. The idea was to take a possession away from the Rams' high-powered offense. It worked. Rob Kelly recovered in front a stunned Rams front line. From that point on, New Orleans took the fight to St. Louis on its home field.

There have been bigger victories in Saints history, but none more unlikely. The Saints were two-touchdown underdogs and playing their first game without tailback Ricky Williams and quarterback Jeff Blake.

In his first career start, backup quarterback Aaron Brooks ran for two touchdowns and passed for another in leading a collection of unsung reserves to big play after big play in a stirring upset for the team's 200th victory.

The Saints' defense, receiving key contributions from reserves Fred Thomas and Chris Oldham, rose to the occasion, holding the Rams to a season-low 279 yards and sacking Trent Green six times.

Somehow this patchwork group of unsung heroes played well enough to overcome a team-record 17 penalties and the Rams' explosive offense.

"We shocked the world today," Saints wide receiver Willie Jackson said. "But we didn't shock ourselves."

The victory moved the Saints (8-4) into a first-place tie in the NFC West Division with the Rams (8-4), with

New Orleans holding the tie-breaker advantage by virtue of Sunday's victory. The last time the Saints were atop the division so late in the season was 1991, the only year they won the division.

"Nobody outside of this (locker) room gave us a chance to win today," Saints right tackle Kyle Turley said. "Everybody had their doubts about what this team could do, about what Aaron Brooks could do, and about what the running game could do. But we know what we have here. We came to play today."

The precocious Brooks completed 17 of 29 passes for 190 yards and looked like a 10-year veteran on the Saints' winning drive. With the sellout crowd of 66,064 roaring in his ears, he calmly drove the Saints 85 yards in 11 plays, then leaped over the goal line from the 1-yard line for the go-ahead touchdown with 3:50 remaining.

"Aaron can play," wide receiver Joe Horn said. "He stayed poised. He stayed under control. And that gave us confidence to see a rookie quarterback smiling."

Defensive tackle La'Roi Glover led another dominant defensive effort with three sacks, including two that forced fumbles inside the Saints' red zone.

Marshall Faulk, the NFL's total yardage leader before missing two games after arthroscopic knee surgery, was held to a season-low 43 totals yards—27 rushing and 16 receiving. Keith Mitchell and Oldham combined to shadow Faulk's every move and never let him turn on the jets.

"We played as well as we probably could play against this football team," Saints coach Jim Haslett said. "Our defense played great red-zone defense. You can't get much better than that."

Saints linebackers coach John Bunting experienced a wild worst-to-first Super Bowl ride in St. Louis the previous season. After the upset of the Rams, he started getting that same feeling from the unheralded and undaunted New Orleans Saints.

"What I felt with the Rams a year ago, I felt in (the Saints) locker room today," Bunting said.

Finally!
December 30, 2000: Saints 31, Rams 28

The ball squirted through Az-Zahir Hakim's fingers, and for a breathless split-second, time stood still at the Superdome.

As the football nestled in Brian Milne's gut at the Rams' 18-yard line, the collective breath of 64,900 shell-shocked fans burst into a relieved and redemptive roar.

"Back at Penn State, the running backs go through a fumble drill where you're taught to get on the ball in a cradle position," said Milne, an unheralded back-up full back. "As soon as I saw the ball slip through his hands, that's what I was thinking about doing. When I got my hands on it, I was squeezing it as tight as I could. If he gets it back, it could have been a different story."

With one wayward bounce, the Saints eradicated 34 years of frustration and the defending Super Bowl champions in an exhilarating 31-28 victory in the wild-card play-offs at the Superdome.

Milne's fumble recovery with 1:43 remaining killed the Rams' furious comeback hopes, preserved the first playoff victory in club history and extended the team's improbable dream season for one more week.

"Take that curse and stick it," Saints assistant head coach Rick Venturi said inside the exuberant Saints locker room afterward.

Jim Haslett and Norman Hand celebrate the franchise's first playoff win, a 31-28 victory against the Rams at the Superdome in 2000. *Eliot Kamenitz/The Times-Picayune*

If not for Milne's recovery, it might not have happened. The Saints appeared on the verge of burying the Rams after opening a 31-7 lead with less than 12 minutes remaining on a pair of Aaron Brooks to Willie Jackson touchdown passes.

But after being bottled up for the first three quarters, the Rams unleashed their high-powered passing attack and scored three touchdowns in a head-spinning seven minutes to make it 31-28 with 2:36 to play. Their final chance to pull out the miracle died with Hakim's fumble.

"We just dug ourselves too big a hole," Rams coach Mike Martz said. "I'm disappointed, very disappointed."

Milne's heroics were fitting. A free-agent pickup who spent most of the season as the reserve fullback, he was one of several second-stringers and former scout-teamers who took turns in the spotlight.

Playing with a patchwork secondary of "guys that weren't even an idea in Thibodaux," according to Venturi, the Saints intercepted Kurt Warner three times and pressured him relentlessly. Strong safety Sammy Knight led the effort with two interceptions, four pass deflections and five tackles.

The defense held Marshall Faulk to 24 rushing yards one week after surrendering 220 to him on the very same field.

"Their pride was hurt and they responded," Zook said.

The win earned the Saints a berth in the divisional round of the NFC playoffs, where they were thrashed 34-16 at Minnesota. But the loss could not take away the joy and redemption fans experienced that Sunday against St. Louis.

"I'm happy for the fans of this city because I know how long they've waited," he said. "What makes it so special is how special this bunch of guys are. They know how to take adversity in stride and go on. We beat a great football team today."

Oops! They Did It Again
October 28, 2001: Saints 34, Rams 31

Kyle Turley was mad as hell and he wasn't going to take it anymore.

He'd just endured one of the most embarrassing halves of football in his career. The Rams blistered the Saints with a pair of touchdowns in the first four minutes of the game and rolled to a 24-6 lead at the break.

The Greatest Show on Turf was living up to its billing. Tight end counters. Reverses. Wide receiver-option passes. The Rams threw Mad Mike Martz's entire playbook at the Saints in the first half and it all worked.

With heavy metal band Pantera coursing through his headphones, Turley nearly tore up the locker room at halftime. In an emotional moment, he challenged his teammates to give it all they had in the final 30 minutes.

Coach Jim Haslett then took the floor.

"I told them (at halftime) it's a 60-minute game," Haslett said. "They're getting bullshit plays on us. If that's how they're going to play, then we should just keep going out and playing our game and we'll win this game. And that's what we did."

Embarrassed and infuriated, the Saints stole "The Show" in the second half with one of the most stunning, exciting comebacks in club history.

The Saints stormed past the error-riddled Rams with a 25-point third quarter, held off a furious fourth-quarter rush and finally put them away on John Carney's 27-yard field goal with one second remaining to cap an exhilarating 34-31 victory.

During the improbable second-half turnaround, the Saints (4-2) forced six turnovers, and Aaron Brooks passed for three touchdowns to rally the visitors to the third-biggest comeback in club history.

"We knew, at some point, the way they play ball would slowly fade away," guard Wally Williams said. "They like to do a lot of running down the field, receivers high-fiving and that sort of thing. We knew that at some point what we do was going to slowly but surely take over the game."

The victory raised the Saints' record to 4-2, but they would go on to lose their final four games and finish the season at 7-9. The upset of the Rams, though, served as another high point in the escalating rivalry between the two clubs.

"Everyone thought it was going to be a blowout," Saints defensive tackle Norman Hand said. "My wife didn't even give us a chance to win this football game. I can call her and rub her face in it."

As he exited the jubilant Saints locker room, wide receiver Joe Horn compared the win to another great sports upset.

"(Remember) Rocky V, when Rocky hit (Ivan) Drago and he started bleeding," Horn said. "And he went back to his corner and his manager said, 'He's bleeding, Rock, he's bleeding. He's human.' They're human. They're not robots that can't be beat. They can be beaten, and today it showed."

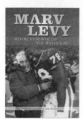

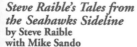
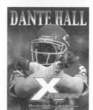